13 Sci-Fi S

Paul Groves and Nigel Grimshaw

Edward Arnold

©Paul Groves and Nigel Grimshaw 1979

First published 1979 by
Edward Arnold (Publishers) Ltd
41 Bedford Square, London WC1B 3DQ

British Library Cataloguing in Publication Data

Groves, Paul
   13 sci-fi stories.
   1. Readers
   I. Grimshaw, Nigel
   428'.6   PE1121

   ISBN 0-7131-0327-2

Set in 12-14 pt VIP Baskerville by Preface Ltd, Salisbury, Wilts, printed in Great Britain by Unwin Brothers Ltd, The Gresham Press, Old Woking, Surrey, and bound by W. H. Ware & Sons Ltd, Clevedon, Avon.

Contents

To The Teacher

This collection of original science fiction stories is written in language simple enough to bring it within the reading range of most pupils. Like most science fiction, these tales are speculative, sometimes sheer flights of fancy and sometimes not. They deal with visitants from other planets, time travel, expeditions to other worlds, some consequences of technology and a possible shape of a future society. Some take a much less serious view of things than others.

Each story is accompanied by questions which examine first the reader's depth of comprehension and go on to ask about the wider implications of the material and the pupil's experience associated with it. There are questions on language usage, spelling and orthography and suggestions for various kinds of creative written work. As the questions range from the simple to the more demanding the book seems suitable for mixed ability classes.

Each story is divided up by * * * * marks, suggesting where the teacher might like to pause and to invite the class to predict as a group the next turn of events in the plot.

The Hunter

Davies fell on one knee. Was that a stag behind that bush? No, it was something smaller, a wildcat or something. He rose and dusted his knee.

Davies was on a hunting trip in the Highlands of Scotland. He was on his own. He had been invited on shooting parties but he preferred to be on his own. There was more of a thrill on your own: just yourself and the quarry; the eternal battle between man and nature.

This time he was after a stag. He was not interested in venison. What he wanted was a fine pair of antlers to decorate the hall of his new house.

He would have to go higher up the mountain. Down here he was downwind of any possible stags. If he could get higher without being seen he would be upwind.

What was that? This time he flung himself on the ground. It was bigger than a wildcat. No, it was a sheep coming from behind that bush; one that had strayed away from the herd.

* * * *

As he fell the thing overhead in the cloud covering was hovering silently. He did not see it and could not sense it—yet it was directly over his head. Inside the thing were four creatures. Two were at the controls: two were watching him.

'Nit fol yak,' said one of the watchers.

'Talk human language of area 67,' came the rejoinder from the red-coloured creature at the controls. 'It is useful practice.'

'Sorry,' said the watcher. 'It is human. It is male, judging

1

from the dress. Just under two metres high. Instructions, please.'

'Observe.'

* * * *

Davies got up and stalked through the scrub. He could not get higher unobserved. He would just have to move quickly and hide up for an hour or two. He would go up to the outcrop and keep watch. He should be upwind there.

'Human is running. Strides of one metre. Breathing hard. Instructions, please.'

'Observe.'

After about twenty minutes of hard going Davies reached the outcrop. Now he had a panoramic view of the mountain. Any deer would probably come out of the forest on the left and cross to the right-hand forest. He had seen them do this before.

'Complexion red. Pulse rate dropping to 120. Is sitting in a crouched position. Instructions, please.'

'Observe.'

* * * *

Davies checked for range. He judged it to be about 400 metres. He would have to allow a fair bit for the wind coming over his left shoulder.

'Human is raising the shooting stick. Pointing it due south. Pulse rate still dropping. Breathing less hard. Instructions, please.'

'Observe.'

Davies took out his pipe and lit it. Now he was upwind he could risk it. He might have a long wait and a pipe was a comfort. He was certain the deer would cross sometime. It was the rutting season. There should be many fine stags.

* * * *

'Smoke coming from human. Is the sun burning him up?'

'No, it is the human habit to inhale the smoke of dead leaves.'

'Sorry, I did not know.'

2

'Consult your human manual more closely and thoroughly.'

'Sorry.'

'Observe.'

Davies looked around. It was cloudy yet there was no sign of rain as yet. Visibility was so good and sharp that it was sure to rain later in the day. He hoped the deer would cross before then. He liked this. There was probably no other being within twenty miles. He felt like a king, high up on a throne, surveying the land below. He took out a sandwich.

'Human eating large object ten centimetres by fifteen centimetres. It is far too big for his mouth. How does he get it in?'

'That is a sandwich made from bread. Once more consult your human manual more thoroughly.'

'Sorry.'

'You have not given me his weight yet.'

'Sorry. Eighty kilograms.'

'Observe.'

* * * *

Yes, they were coming. Davies could see a lead deer coming out of the forest. It was looking round for danger. Three more appeared. Yes, they were going to cross. The first animal was a most magnificent stag. He sighted and held his finger ready to squeeze the trigger.

'All information recorded.'

'Right distance please.'

'Five hundred and twenty-one metres, six centimetres, two millimetres.'

'Exterminate.'

As Davies squeezed the trigger he was burned to a small pile of ashes. No shot rang out and the deer crossed safely to the forest.

Think It Over

What was Davies hunting?
Where was he hunting?
What did Davies particularly enjoy about hunting?
Why did he want to get upwind of possible stags?
What animals fed on the mountain?
What is hovering over Davies' head?
What prevented him from seeing it?
Why are Davies's strides not longer?
How much of the mountain could Davies see from the outcrop? How do you know?
How do you know Davies has been on the mountain before?
What sort of information can the creatures get about Davies? What do they not know?
How do you know the creatures have visited Earth before?
What told Davies that there would be rain later?
For what reason, do you think, did the creatures exterminate Davies?

Do You Know?

What is venison?
Where do you find wildcats?
What other ways are there of hunting stags?
What other kinds of wild animal in England are hunted for their meat?
Where are the highest mountains in Britain?
What might the ship hovering over Davies have looked like?
What might Area 67 be?
What is an outcrop?
Why do deer move from place to place?
What is a person's normal pulse rate? Can you find out what yours is at this moment? Is exercise the only thing that can send up your pulse rate? What else can do that?

Is 400 metres more or less than a mile? By how much?

Why does he have to allow for the wind?

Is it easy or difficult to fire a rifle when you are breathing hard and quickly? Why do you think so?

What is the rutting season?

What do you call a female deer?

Why would the UFO creatures require a human manual?

What other signs of approaching rain are there?

When have you felt like a king or queen?

Why is the line: '. . . no other being within twenty miles' ironic?

Why is the title of the story ironic?

How might the creatures have killed Davies?

Using Words

What words might describe a stag?

'on his own'. How many different ways are there of saying this?

List the names of the meat from these animals: sheep (two kinds), bullock, calf.

'pair of'. What other terms mean two of something?

What kind of bird usually hovers?

Invent a sentence of your own in space language.

What is the difference between *practice* and *practise*?

'It is male'. What would be a more usual way of saying this?

Use 'stalked' in a sentence of your own.

'outcrop'. How many words can you think of that begin *out*?

'a panoramic view'. Put this more simply.

Use *probably*, correctly spelt, in a sentence of your own.

What is the opposite of *inhale*?

'visibility'. How many words like this, which are often used in weather forecasts, can you think of?

What is the Northern name for a sandwich? Where does the word *sandwich* come from?

Write Now

Draw the UFO and the creature watching Davies.

Describe one of the watchers.

Write the news item with the headline: 'Hunter Missing'.

Write a poem called 'The Watcher'.

Write a story of a man who escapes from people—police or soldiers—who are hunting him.

Do the creatures in this story go back to their home planet and report? Do they land on Earth after Davies has been killed? Write an account of what happens next.

Sting

Cyril Wicks leapt back from the hive. The bee had got under the net and stung him on the shoulder through his shirt. He was used to bee stings. He had probably been stung over a hundred times in his life as a bee keeper. But this sting really hurt; it was like toothache in the shoulder.

But in spite of the pain his eyes shone. He had done it. His work of the last few years had not been wasted: he had bred a big bee. There had been the careful selection of strains to get the biggest bee possible; and then the master stroke: feeding them on blood. He had tried both dried sheep's blood and horse's blood; both seemed effective.

* * * *

He went inside to remove the sting. It was difficult but he got it out in two pieces. He placed them together; the sting measured two centimetres in length.

Down on his lonely Cornwall farm the chance of people getting stung was remote. He could go on and develop the bees. They would not go more than a mile or two from his hives in search of pollen. His nearest neighbour was four miles away. No one should know about it until he sold his secrets to a honey manufacturer. He envisaged bee farms with bees kept in giant sheds like the factory farming of pigs and cattle. It could make him rich and famous.

* * * *

And that, with Cyril Wicks rich, could have been the end of the story. But his nearest neighbour was also experimenting. He was trying out different weed-killers to kill off some wild flowers that plagued one of his fields some two miles from Cyril Wicks' farm. The flowers seemed immune to normal weed-killer so he had mixed several brands together.

Unknown to both of them the bees, had one very hot day, taken pollen from the flowers of the treated plants. This caused a mutation.

Cyril Wicks had gone down to his hives some months later. He stopped and stared in amazement. There on top of one of the hives were three bees. They measured at least ten centimetres in length. Their bodies were as big as a blackbird's. As he went closer to look, he stepped on a twig. It snapped and frightened the bees which buzzed round him angrily and then came in immediately to the attack on the unfortunate Mr Wicks.

* * * *

The first one stung him in the hand. He looked amazed as the sting went right through his palm and came out the other side. The second bee stung him like a red hot poker on the side of the knee. He collapsed to the ground and watched the third bee buzz over him. It did three circles and came in straight for his stomach. It drove its sting in deep. He twisted in agony for five minutes. Then he lay still.

There were no callers at the remote farm to discover the body. Only the postman called and he put his letters in a box at the end of the lane. It is assumed that the bees fed on the body as it decomposed, and sucked out the blood as only his skeleton was found later. For the bees developed a taste for the human body.

* * * *

The first evidence the public of Cornwall had of the bees was the mysterious death of six cows and a sheep on the neighbouring farm. The vet could not understand the deaths and the giant stings measuring five centimetres.

It was while he was waiting for a report from London that some children saw the bees. They had travelled ten miles from Mr Wicks's farm to the coast. The children were dive-bombed while bathing. They were able to get into the water and frighten the bees away with splashing. At first the children's account was put down to exaggeration by their parents from London.

Then a tractor driver was found dead with a sting in his throat and half of the neck eaten away.

* * * *

Nothing happened for the next few weeks but then the weather was very cold and dull.

On the first of June the town of Polven had just breakfasted. The milkmen and postmen were on their rounds; children were making their way to school; early morning shoppers were out. Then, from the south, came a faint hum. It was like a low note played on a cello. It got louder and louder. A policeman got off his bike and was looking up, expecting to see an aeroplane flying low. He suddenly saw this dark cloud. He took it at first to be a vast cloud of flies but soon he could see that it was a swarm of bees; not ordinary bees but giant bees following a queen. Before he could give any alarm they had passed over his head in the direction of the town centre. As they did so, they blotted out the sun. Being a brave man, he did not dive for cover but radioed his station.

* * * *

At the police station they thought the officer was drunk and called him back in off duty. But it would have made no difference if they had believed him; there was nothing they could do to stop what followed.

The bees flew straight to the centre of the town and settled on the town hall. Startled shoppers watched them crawl all over the building. They were hypnotized by the sight before attempting to escape from the area.

The bees might have stayed there round the queen but a car coming down the road back-fired. This startled the bees and they rose in an angry cloud and attacked everything that moved.

* * * *

9

They buzzed down on cars and buses and any unfortunate pedestrians. Some shop keepers did not get their doors closed quickly enough; office workers had windows open; so the bees were soon inside as well as out.

Thirty people were stung to death; a hundred were injured, some from crashing cars. Several old people died of fright.

Eventually, after an attack lasting fifteen minutes, the bees flew back to the town hall. The police called in the army who kept watch on the bees from armoured cars and tanks while the whole town was evacuated. This took all morning as old and sick people had to be moved by ambulance. All the time the worry was: Would the bees attack again?

* * * *

At last it was done. Then crop-spraying planes and helicopters flew over the town and 'bombed' the bees with poisonous gas. The watchers from the tanks saw the bees drop off the town hall one by one.

Two weeks were given for the gas to clear. Then the bees were swept up in piles. Bee-keepers of the area searched for the queen. She was not found. Had she escaped the gas?

A queen bee can lay up to three thousand eggs a day.

So far no sightings have been made of her. But then you can never be sure where a queen bee will find a hole or a crevice to make a nest. The whole of Cornwall remains on the alert. Many of the inhabitants of Polven have not returned to their homes. The rest of the country does not sleep easily either.

Think It Over

Was Cyril Wicks used to bee stings?
What was different about this bee sting?
What food had produced this breed of bee?

How big was the sting?
Why were these bees little danger to other people?
What did Cyril Wicks expect to get out of this new breed of bees?
How would the bees be kept?
How did the bees grow even bigger?
How big were the new bees?
Why did the bees attack Mr Wicks?
Why was he not discovered for a long time?
What was particularly alarming about the large bees?
What could the vet not understand?
Who were the next people to see the bees?
How did these people escape attack?
Why were the bees not very active after the death of the tractor driver?
What first alerted the people of Polven to the presence of the bees?
What were the giant bees following when they swarmed?
Who gave the alarm? Why was he not believed?
Why did the people remain on the street and not get under cover?
What angered the bees?
How long did their attack last? What were the casualties?
What did the army do?
How were the bees attacked?
Which bee was not found when the other dead bees were swept up?
What might this mean?

Do You Know?

What are beehives made from?
What should you put on a bee sting?
What do you put on a wasp sting? Does a wasp leave a sting?
How long is a normal bee's sting?

What different kind of bees are there in a hive?
What do bees normally feed on?
What is pollen? Why is a pollen count sometimes given over
the radio?
What are people suffering from, if pollen causes them dis-
tress?
What do you understand by 'factory farming'? How is it
different from normal farming?
What is the smallest British bird? What is the largest?
Why do bees sometimes attack people?
Have you every been stung by an insect? What was your
worst experience with insects? What did you do about it?
Why would the vet have had to examine the dead cattle?
Why do bees swarm?
When did you last see a crowd staring at something? What
was it?

Using Words

List the various 'aches' the body can have.
Use *bred* and *bread* in sentences of your own.
Use *strain* in two different ways.
'the master stroke'. What does this mean?
What is a *mutation*?
Use *palm* in two different ways.
It 'stung him like a red hot poker'. Using the word *like*
describe the feeling of being stung in another way.
'Then he lay still.' What does this really mean?
'dive-bombed'. What is a dive-bomber? Where were they
used?
How many questions are there in this story? Write them out.
'throat' Make a list of *oa* words.
'Before he could give any alarm they had passed over his
head in the direction of the town square.' Complete the
following:
Before the ship landed . . .

Before the gangster could pull the gun . . .
Before I even saw Martin coming . . .
Use the following words, correctly spelt, in sentences of your
own: probably, neighbour, immediately, exaggeration,
aeroplane.

Write Now

Write your own story about a plague of insects.
You invent some food that increases the size of all creatures.
  You leave it in your back garden. What happens?
In play-form write the conversation that the policeman who
  saw the bees had with his station OR an officer radios
  back to the police station what is happening at the town
  hall.
Find out what you can about bees and write a short article
  about them.
The queen has escaped the gas. Write a story of what hap-
  pens next summer.
Write a poem called 'Bees on a Summer's Day'.
Write the newspaper report that appeared in the *Polven
  News*.

Tree Food Is Good For You

The planet Fraja has an Earth-type climate. It has no wild animals and the native Frajian people are friendly. Why, then, have no Earth-men settled there? Let us look at the facts.

There was a glint of silver in the clear blue sky of the planet Fraja. The four Frajians, Dugg, Mugg, Lugg and Wugg, watched it. It grew larger and began to descend.

'A bird,' said Mugg.

'A space-ship,' Dugg corrected him. He was the clever one.

'It's going to land,' said Lugg.

'Oooh! Oooh! How exciting!' gasped Wugg. She was always excitable.

The silver glint grew larger still. Dugg had been right. It was a space-ship. A pillar of fire shimmered from its tail. It descended gracefully on this and came to rest, gleaming, on the plain not far away. The Frajians waited expectantly.

A door opened in the side of the ship. A ladder slid out and landed on the ground. Four figures began to walk down the ladder.

'People like us,'' said Dugg.

'They don't look like us,' Lugg objected.

'They are like us,' Dugg told him. 'I can tell.'

'They look nice,' said Wugg.

'What do you mean, "nice"?' said Mugg. 'They are not for eating. Eating people is wrong.'

'She didn't mean that,' said Dugg.

'I didn't mean that,' Wugg agreed.

'But Mugg is right,' argued Lugg. 'Eating people is not healthy. Only tree food is healthy.'

'Tree food is good for you.' Mugg said solemnly.

'Shut up, you two,' Dugg ordered. 'Don't be silly. Just shut up.' They obeyed.

* * * *

The four human beings, Captain Robinson, Engineer Jones, Doctor Smith and Doctor Brown, approached and came within speaking distance. The two parties stood for a moment in silence, looking at each other. The Frajians looked like large Easter eggs. Their skin was bright with many different colours. They stood on four stubby legs and they had four arms apiece. They each had two large eyes a little more than halfway up their bodies. The human beings looked like human beings in zip-up silver suits.

Captain Robinson switched on his Translating Machine and spoke into it. The words were immediately translated into the Frajian language.

'We come in peace,' were the words that the Frajians heard.

'They come in peace,' said Dugg.

'I knew they would,' said Wugg. 'I told you they were nice.'

'Why are they carrying those big, shiny things in their hands?' asked Mugg.

'I will ask them,' said Dugg. He did.

'These weapons?' said Captain Robinson. 'They're purely for defence.'

He switched off his Translating Machine and spoke to his crew. The Frajians waited patiently.

* * * *

'They're a queer-looking bunch,' he said.

'I've seen queerer,' Engineer Jones decided. 'They seem harmless.'

'I'll examine their make-up,' Doctor Smith said and moved in with his Examining Machine. He ran it quickly over Wugg's body. Wugg giggled, wriggling slightly. Doctor Smith stepped back and consulted the dials.

'You are brave,' breathed Doctor Brown. She admired Doctor Smith.

'It was nothing,' Smith told her. 'All in the line of duty.' He nodded wisely. 'These creatures are very like us,' he reported to Captain Robinson. 'They have blood. They're very like Earth mammals.'

'I expected it,' said Robinson. 'The planet's got an Earth-type climate. It figures.'

'But are they really like us?' Jones objected. 'They could be just a type of animal.'

'We'll find out.' Captain Robinson switched on his Translating Machine again. 'Are you the highest form of life on this planet?' he asked.

'What?' said Dugg

'Do you run this planet?' Robinson explained. 'Are you sort of in charge of things here?'

'What?' Dugg repeated.

'Let me try.' Doctor Smith took the Translating Machine and asked. 'Do you live in towns?'

'Towns?' said Dugg.

'We live under the trees,' Lugg said.

'So that we can get tree food easily,' Wugg added.

'Tree food is good for you,' Mugg told them, wanting to be helpful.

'Have some,' said Wugg, offering a piece.

'Thank you,' said Miss Brown politely. 'Is it nice?'

'Not very,' said Mugg. 'But it's good for you.'

* * * *

'Let's get back to the ship,' Robinson decided. 'We can talk things over. We can have a look at that stuff, too.'

They went back to the ship. The Frajians watched them go and began to munch pieces of tree food.

Captain Robinson and his crew were an ESPTC or an Earth Scouting Party (Twenty-third Century). There were many such parties and it was their job to explore unknown planets. Earth's population was continually growing and it was necessary to find new planets on which people could settle. Fraja seemed ideal. But, like any other planet, it had to be thoroughly researched first.

The crew went to work. They got their planet buggy out of the space ship and roamed the plains of Fraja. They even examined the sea as well as they could. They found no other life form to which they could talk. They found no other life form as large as Dugg and Mugg and the others. It certainly looked as though Dugg and Mugg and any others like them were the highest life form on the planet.

* * * *

They examined the tree food. That was puzzling. It looked just like wood such as is found on Earth. It smelt like wood. It even tasted like wood. Extensive scientific tests seemed to prove that it was wood.

'But that's just a detail,' Captain Robinson told them on the third day. He passed his hand wearily over his brow. He was not feeling too well. 'We know a good deal now about this planet. We know our next step. Those egg-like creatures are people. Our orders are to make friends with the inhabitants of any new planet. We are supposed to give them gifts. We introduce them to our civilisation.'

'Where do we start?' asked Engineer Jones. 'There's a lot of civilisation they don't know about, it seems to me.'

'They do have a very low intelligence,' Robinson agreed. 'But that's all to the good, isn't it? They'll be grateful for whatever we can give them. They have no fire, they have no machines.'

'They don't need fire,' said Doctor Smith. 'They don't cook that wood stuff that they eat.'

'That's it!' Captain Robinson snapped his fingers. 'Food! We'll introduce them to Earth-type food. After that wood of theirs, anything ought to taste good to them.'

* * * *

So Dr Brown pulled a few selector buttons on the Food-

17

Producing Machine and came up with a plate of bacon and eggs, caviare and some Chinese chow mein.

But the Frajians would not be tempted.

'We must only eat tree food,' Lugg explained.

'Nothing but tree food,' Mugg told them.

'Every day and nothing else,' Wugg agreed.

'Tree food is good for you,' Mugg said and shyly offered Miss Brown a piece. She took it and, as he seemed to be watching her, she ate some of it.

'Rubbish!' Dugg suddenly burst out. 'Mugg! You are boring! You are boring because you are superstitious. Our rules say that we must eat only tree food. But a time comes when a brave and clever Frajian must change the rules. I will eat Earth food. It smells delicious.' And in rapid succession he ate the bacon and eggs, the caviare and the Chinese chow mein.

But, in spite of his example, none of the other three Frajians would eat any of the Earth-type food. And it went on like that for three days. Miss Brown tried to tempt the Frajians with all kinds of things from fish and chips to Japanese suki-yaki. She even ate a little of the Frajian tree food herself to show there were no hard feelings. Only Dugg ate all she gave him. The others simply refused.

* * * *

It was on the third day that Dugg fell over and lay motionless. At almost the same time Captain Robinson groaned and toppled to the ground. Engineer Jones sat down, too, holding his head. When he touched his hair, a lot of it fell out. The Frajians made sorrowing and sympathetic noises. In their very simple way they tried to explain.

'They have not eaten their tree food,' said Lugg. 'That is why they are ill.'

'What are you talking about?' asked Miss Brown shortly. She was not feeling too good herself.

'There is a thing in the air on Fraja,' Wugg explained. 'It attacks you and makes you ill.'

'But only if you don't eat tree food,' Mugg added. 'You must always eat only tree food. Tree food is g – – –'

'All right! All right!' Miss Brown snapped. 'I'm beginning to understand. Help me to get these three back to the ship.'

By that time Doctor Smith had fallen on his face, too.

* * * *

The three Earth men and Miss Brown recovered completely on their voyage back to Earth. So did Dugg after large doses of tree food. Extensive research was carried out after they got back to Earth. But the matter still rests there.

There is no secret ingredient in Frajian tree food. It is just like Earth wood. And that is the difficulty.

Fraja is a perfect planet for Earth people to settle on. There are no dangerous animals there and only one disease.

But, if you go to Fraja, you must always eat Frajian tree food—or wood. If, as you must, you eat nothing but Frajian tree food all the time, you will, like Miss Brown, suffer from terrible stomach ache. Wood is not nourishing. In the end you will starve to death.

If you do not eat Frajian tree food and nothing but Frajian tree food all the time, you will be attacked by the dreaded Frajian illness. At first your hair will drop out and your toe nails will fall off. You will suffer from fainting fits. Later, the illness will kill you.

It is a problem that, so far, no one has solved. Up to now, no Earth-men have settled on Fraja.

Think It Over

What is odd about the Frajian names?

What powered the space ship?

Do Frajians eat people? What do they eat?

What shows you that the Earthmen were careful when they landed on a new planet?

What do Frajians look like?

How can Captain Robinson talk to the Frajians?

19

How do you know that this is not the first planet the Earth
people have visited?
Why might Wugg have giggled when she was examined?
How do the Frajians resemble mammals?
Why is Captain Robinson scouting for new planets?
Why do the Frajians not need fire? How do you know that
their civilisation was not very advanced?
How did the Earth party go on to explore the planet?
When is the first time you notice the effect Fraja has on
Earthmen?
Why does Dugg eat the Earth food? Was Captain Robin-
son's idea of giving the Frajians Earth food a good one?
Why?
Why was Miss Brown not affected by the disease as much as
the others?
How did the Frajians feel about eating their tree food?
Can you put into one sentence the problem Earthmen would
have if they went to live on Fraja?

Do You Know?

What are the vital substances that make life on our planet
possible?
Can you name four planets in the solar system? Which
planet might be the first to be the first to be explored by a
manned landing?
What is rocket fuel made of? If you don't know, can you find
out?
What kind of food is good for a person normally? What
kinds of food are supposed to be bad for you? What do you
call somebody who eats people?
What years would the 23rd century cover?
Which, do you think, is the queerest-looking Earth mam-
mal? Why do you think so?
Name another class of animal beside mammals. What kind
of mammals live in the sea?

What is the highest form of life on Earth? What is the lowest
   form?
Which is the least intelligent of the Frajians? What makes
   you think so?
Which country of the world has the largest population?
Name two of the earliest inventions of man. What would you
   say are the main gifts of our civilisation?
Who is the politest member of Captain Robinson's party and
   how do you know?
Do you approve of the mixture of foods Miss Brown tempted
   the Frajians with? What would you have offered them?

Using Words

What is caviare?
What does H. G. Wells call a person from Mars?
Invent some other names for the Frajians.
'Tree Food is Good for You'. Write down three TV slogans.
Use *piece* and *peace* in sentences of your own.
What does a doctor examine your chest with? Write down
   another word with the same ending.
'They look nice'. What other word could she have used
   instead of *nice* to make her meaning clearer?
'Shut up' What would be two other ways of saying this?
'It figures.' Explain what Robinson means.
Where did the word *buggy*, meaning a mode of transport,
   come from?
Use these words in sentences of your own: expectantly,
   continually, inhabitant, civilisation.

Write Now

Invent and describe a planet where living conditions would
   be perfect.

Draw a Frajian.

Write a poem called, 'Feeling Ill'.

In play-form write (a) what the humans talked about on their way back to Earth, OR (b) what the Frajians said to Dugg after he recovered, OR (c) what the scouting party talked about to the inhabitants of the next planet they visited.

The exploration team have all kinds of special and useful machines. What kind of extraordinary machine would you like to own and what would you do with it?

Timeslip

The cave was huge and dark. The floor was wet and there was a steady sound of trickling water. The only light came from a crude lamp. In its glow could be seen the many forms of sleepers, slumped against the walls. They were all ragged and dirty. Some cried out in their sleep. One man, however, was awake. In the lamp light, he was carving a message on the wall of the cave. It was a long message and he had evidently been working on it for a long time.

Painfully, letter by letter, using a sharp-pointed stone, he wrote another line. And then another. And then a third. He put down the stone and picked up the lamp. Holding it close to the wall, he read over what he had written. It took him some time. He nodded at last. 'Finished!' he breathed. His face was pale and haggard in the flickering light. He blew out the lamp and set it down on a rock. Then he curled up on the floor and was immediately asleep. This is what he had written.

* * * *

My name is Michael Clegg. In another time I used to be a scientist. I was a member of Norman Washbourne's team. I was the first man ever to travel in time. That is—as far as I know. There are many different streams of time. I found that out.

It was Norman Washbourne who discovered time travel. All of us in his team had been working on the idea for years. Until the meteorite, we had failed. That landed in Australia. When it was examined, three or four strange crystals were discovered. They had very unusual properties. Norman Washbourne had the genius to realise what they meant. He thought they would give us time-travel. And he was right. But it will not be discovered again. The time machine has disappeared for him. And for me.

Norman Washbourne made a time machine and I destroyed it. I destroyed the possibility of time-travel. I hope I destroyed it for ever. In this cave that is something to be proud of. I have found out what terrible things happen if a man travels in time.

* * * *

I used to live in a place called England. I lived in the twentieth century. The year was 1997. Where I am now, I do not know. I think the place may be the same. Perhaps the year is still the same. I have no way of finding out.

It was summer. For a week we had made the time machine work. All the experiments had gone well. We had sent objects back a short distance in time and recovered them. On the last experiment we had sent back a monkey in time. It had returned, unharmed. Now we were planning to send a man.

We were all very pleased. We had a party that week-end to celebrate. And I drank too much. On my way home, I had an accident on the road. I killed a man. The police let me go on bail but I knew I would have to go to prison. I knew that my career was ruined. I knew that I would have no part of Norman Washbourne's triumph. I would not share the secrets of time-travel.

* * * *

I was standing in the laboratory, looking at the machine. I suppose I was saying goodbye to all I had hoped for and dreamed of. And then the idea came to me. I thought it would save me. I saw the way to escape both punishment and ruin.

I knew how to work the machine. I would go back in time to the scene of the accident. But there would be no accident. I would be very careful of that. I would alter the past and then I would be safe. I thought it would be easy. It was. Dreadfully easy.

I got into the machine. I set the controls for a time ten minutes before the accident and started. For a short while I travelled through a grey blur, dizzily. When I stopped and got out, there was a blank. I felt a wrenching pain. But I was back at the party. And I remembered.

I got into my car. Knowing what might happen had sobered me. I drove slowly through the streets. I came to the scene of the accident. This time I braked. There was no accident. But I never left that scene. In the moment when it should have happened, I was thrown into another world.

* * * *

I have worked it out since. I have had a lot of time to think things over. I tried to change the past. That has brought me here.

Time is not like a single river. Time is a matter of many streams. In time there are many worlds, each lying parallel to one another. When I lived in England in 1997, I was living in one possible world. When I tried to change the past, I jolted myself into a different time stream.

In this time stream there is a different history. This land—and it may be England still—has been invaded by an alien race from the stars. They have conquered all the populations of Earth. They have forced them to work as slaves. I have been here now for several years. I have had time to find out many things. Earth's population may have other work in other places. I know that I must work here in slavery until I die.

Who will read this? For whom will it be a warning? Only myself. None of the others working here would have understood what I have to tell them. But I needed to put it down. Perhaps it was a way—maybe it was the only way—to stop myself from going mad.

The sleepers in the cave groaned in their dreams. Michael

Clegg slept without a sound. All his nightmares happened when he was awake.

Think It Over

Why are the people in the cave?
Why do some of them cry out in their sleep?
How did the scientists manage to make a time machine?
What happened to the time machine?
How did Clegg know that the machine would work for him?
What happened after the party?
What effect would Clegg's going to prison have on his work?
How did he try to escape his punishment?
What happened when he reached the scene of the accident again?
What effect did the actual travelling through time have on him?
What was the terrible result of his travelling through time?
What is different about the new time stream?
Explain the last line of the story.

Do You Know?

What did early man put on cave walls?
What sort of work might Clegg and the others have been doing?
Is there any significance in the fact that they were in a cave?
How long do you think it has taken Clegg to scratch out this story? What kind of stone might he have been using for his writing? What very soft stone is often used to write with?
How might he have made his lamp?
What is a meteorite? What is a meteor? (You will need a dictionary.)
What happens to drunken drivers when they are caught?

What can you buy in the form of crystals?
What is the population of the Earth?
What other kinds of animal do scientists use in experiments?
Name some of the nations in the past who have kept slaves.

Using Words

What is bail?
Had Clegg murdered the man in the road? What is that
   crime called?
'message'. How many words do you know that end -*age*?
'trickling water'. How many words can you find whose
   sound describes water?
How do you look if you look haggard?
'unusual properties', Explain this. If a house agent used the
   word *property* what does he mean?
Write in words the centuries between the years 2000 and
   3000
'wrenching' Make a list of words that begin *wr-*.
Use these words, correctly spelt, in sentences of your own:
   experiment, career, alter, alien, population, immediately.

Write Now

Describe what Michael Clegg does during the day.
If you could travel back through time, what time in history
   would you like to live in and why?
You go forward in time. Describe some of the changes that
   you notice.
Clegg manages to escape from the cave. Is he recaptured?
   Or, does he manage to find his way back to his own time
   again?
Your are living at the time when the alien creatures invade
   Earth. Describe how they come, what they look like and
   how they conquer the planet.
Write a poem called 'The Cave'.

The Big Bubbles

Some say it couldn't have happened. Others say there must be a natural explanation about it all. Both the scientists and the military have been over the spot. They could find nothing. All that we are left with is Bob White's story. And a strange story it is. The story of a drunken man perhaps?

He was a farm labourer down at Lower Cheney in Somerset. I say 'was' because he has not worked since the incident. He now has to visit the hospital a lot and take bottles of tablets.

It happened one summer day when the corn was ripening in the fields. Bob White was weeding a cabbage field. The day was very hot. The trees in the distance were shimmering in the heat; there were pools on the roads. He paused often to mop his forehead.

The rest of the village was at dinner. The doctor was snatching a hurried lunch; the vicar had just left the church and was enjoying cold chicken; the farmer was in the pub as were many of Bob's fellow workers. Bob was doing a spot of overtime to help run his car. It was a peaceful scene with nobody in the lanes: a typical English village on a summer's day.

Bob White stood up once more to wipe his forehead. He was beginning to regret he had decided to work. He would have loved to have been down at the pub with his fellows having a shandy.

As he stood up he stepped back in amazement. A large object hovered over the village. It was circular but it was about the size of the village football field or more. Yet despite its size it made no sound.

* * * *

Had he got a touch of the sun? He blinked and pinched himself. No. There it was, blocking out the sun so that a huge shadow lay over the village.

It was ribbed like a rubber tyre; in the ribs were portholes or windows. It glowed with a kind of orange light.

He wanted to run away but he stood fixed to the spot and watched. As he did so a large bubble came out from underneath the UFO and slowly floated down. There was no wind and it floated straight down. Then came a second bubble to join it. It was like a child blowing bubbles from a pipe. A third bubble followed.

* * * *

The first bubble came down on the church. It was so big that it covered it. It looked as though the church was in a glass case. It enclosed the entire church including the steeple.

The second bubble came down on the pub which stood by itself next to the village green. It covered it including the sign outside.

The third was a massive bubble; it covered the entire village main street consisting of ten houses. The fourth bubble which had since emerged from the UFO covered the farm.

* * * *

As quickly as they had floated down they started to rise. First the bubble with the church inside it. Bob White gasped as this huge building was lifted off the ground as lightly as a blade of grass. Then the bubble with the pub inside it floated up. Then the massive bubble rose and within, trapped inside, the village main street. The farm followed quickly after.

The light from the UFO had changed to a light green and Bob White swore he saw things like big eyes looking out of the portholes.

As the bubbles rose Bob White saw people run out of the pub and the houses on the village street. They fell out of the doors and rolled round in a struggling heap at the bottom of the bubbles.

Quickly the bubbles reached the UFO. A gap opened in the ribbed side and the bubbles looked as though they were sucked in. The light changed to orange. Now there was no trace of the church, the pub, the street or the farm.

*. * * *

Bob White kept looking as he stood rooted to the spot. Now another bubble came out. It was much smaller than the others. And it was coming down towards him!

He took to his heels and ran. He stopped once to look back. The bubble was bouncing up and down on the spot where he had been, like a ball. He turned and ran again. He was a good sportsman and fit but each time he looked over his shoulder he could see the bubble bouncing after him. There was no doubt that it was getting closer and closer.

He had crossed the cabbage field and was running down the side of a field of wheat. Now he could sense that the bubble was right behind him. The village pond suddenly was in front of him; he dived straight in. It was deep and he swam under water. Above him the bubble bounced on the surface a few times. He could not hold his breath much longer; he would have to surface.

* * * *

He came up expecting to be grabbed by the bubble but it had floated away. He could see it floating up to the UFO and its green light. He got out of the pond, shaking with cold and fright. Then he rushed home and drank half a bottle of whisky. The UFO flew off towards Taunton then suddenly disappeared after a sharp upward flight.

Anyway, that is Bob White's story of what happened. You do not have to believe it, except that Lower Cheney is no longer there. All you will see is an empty road and a few trees. You will not see any people, except perhaps Bob

White. He sometimes feels drawn to go back to the village where he was born. He looks very lonely as he walks down the empty street.

Think It Over

What sort of people examined the spot?
Who is the only person who knows the true story?
What is the name of the place?
What effect did the incident have on him?
What kind of day was it when the incident happened?
How many people were outside at the time?
Why was Bob alone in the field?
How big was the object he saw?
What did it look like?
How do you know it was real?
What sort of things came out of the object?
What was the first thing to disappear? What was the fourth?
What did Bob see then?
What happened to all the people who were inside the buildings?
What saved Bob?
In which direction did the UFO fly?
What is there left of the village now?

Do You Know?

Why would people find it difficult to believe Bob's story?
What would they think about him?
Why would it be unjust to think of Bob's story as the story of a drunken man?
What counties in England begin with the letter 'S'?
About what month of the year might it have been? What makes you think so?

What causes 'pools' in the road in summer?
Why might the doctor's lunch have been hurried?
Where does a vicar live?
What is a shandy made from?
Give the names on the signs of three pubs in your area.
Do you know why any one of them is called what it is?
What is the average size of a full-sized football pitch?
Why are tyres normally ribbed? Do different tyres have
    different ribbing for different uses? Explain, if you can.
How big were the creatures in the UFO? What makes you
    think so?
Where is Taunton? Do you know why this story has been set
    in the south-west of England?

Using Words

What is 'the military'? Use it in a sentence of your own.
'Bob White's story'. Which of these needs an apostrophe:
    doctors tablets, vicars lunch, UFOs bubbles, says, sum-
    mers day, Bobs fellow workers?
'field'. List six more *ie* words.
Use 'typical' in a sentence of your own.
'forehead'. Write down six more *fore* words.
What is the difference between 'hovered' and 'hoovered'?
Give two meanings for the word 'circular'.
'as lightly as a blade of grass'. What else could it have been
    as light as? Give three alternatives.
Give two meanings for the word 'rose'.
Punctuate this sentence correctly: 'Now there was no sight of
    the harpooner the crew the ship or the whale.' You will
    find a sentence like it in the story to check with.
'fit'. How many meanings can this word have? Use each in a
    sentence of your own.

Write Now

A ship is found at sea. There is food still on the tables but all the crew have disappeared. Can you think of an explanation for this?

Describe a hot summer day as if you were a farm worker working in a field.

In play-form invent the conversation some of the captured villagers might have when they find themselves on board the UFO.

You are walking in the country one day when you are chased by a strange flying object. What happens and how do you escape?

Describe a typical English village. Draw a plan, if you like.

Draw the UFO and the bubbles.

Write a poem called 'Bubbles'.

You are a TV interviewer questioning Bob White. You doubt his story. List the questions you ask him.

The Greenhouse Children

Peter 33 sucked his B4 tablet. It was pink and sickly. The bell had gone and it was talk time. Meakins was looking hard at him. He had better move. He had to talk to each member of his group on matters of the Party. 'The Cluster' it was called. You spent five minutes with each member of your group. Each talk was monitored by a TV camera and Meakins, Leader 21, gave criticisms on them the next day.

That was how the day started. After a run round the track at 0600 hours, a shower at 0630, Meal One at 0645, the day began at 0715 with The Cluster. Peter 33 hated it.

He had been selected for this school at the age of seven. He was not thirteen. When he was twenty he would leave and take his place in the Ministry of Taxes. He was good at maths.

* * * *

John 24 came over to him for the talk. The camera zoomed in on them. Then, joy, the light on it went out. It was not working. They could talk about anything until the light went on again.

'I've heard another tale of the Outside,' said John 24. The Outside was the world beyond the twenty metre electrified fence that surrounded the school. No one went back to the Outside until they were trained, at the age of twenty. 'They say that boys mix together and are friendly with girls.'

'No!' exclaimed Peter 33. Here the girls were in a separate school compound separated by a solid steel fence. You could only sometimes hear their shouts from a game of hockey or something.

'I did hear they had a sweet thing they could chew on.'

'Not only that,' said John, 'they can smoke as well.' John was a fund of knowledge about the Outside. He leaned closer. They could see Meakins, Leader 21, at the control box trying to get the camera working. 'I think we should try to escape.'

* * * *

'Escape!' gasped Peter. The word had hit him like a medicine ball in the stomach. 'How?'

'I think we could get out in the kitchen waste cart.'

The light went on. John switched the conversation to the Party.

In his small room that night Peter could not sleep. He lay there thinking of John's idea. The rules were that if you could not sleep you rang for a tablet. He kept his eyes tight shut in case the camera was working. To escape to the outside world! Perhaps he could find his mother and father. When he had last heard, at the age of ten, they were still living in the same town. But what if he and John were caught?

* * * *

Rumour had it that Mark 33 had escaped. He was not there one day. When he reappeared he spoke to no one but the leaders. He had been a cheerful, laughing boy but that all stopped. He had to have special tablets at meals and he always disappeared with Meakins after Meal 3.

But the urge to see his mother and father was stronger than his worry about what would happen if they were caught. The problem was when could he and John talk again. It would have to be at night during shower 2. The boys reckoned the running water drowned the sound that went to the microphones.

But he must play safe before he talked with John next. He rang for a tablet.

* * * *

When he came off the running track the next morning, he made sure he showered next to John. But Meakins was there parading up and down. When he got to Meal One, however, he realised that there was a piece of paper in his trouser pocket. He would have to wait till he was in the toilet before he could look at it. John winked at him from another table.

The toilets and the showers were the only places you were not watched by the cameras. There were microphones in there so you could not talk to the next cubicle.

Peter took the note out of his pocket. He had two minutes to look at it during Toilet Two. There were no words on it, just a diagram of the running track and the position of the kitchen and the place the place the waste truck parked in. John had worked out that it was a blind spot for the cameras.

You exercised during the morning jogging session with a different boy each day. After three weeks the time came when he was with John. They jogged round in the normal fashion without speaking, then on the bend they were suddenly away for the waste truck. They had to risk that there were no spies among the boys but you could never tell. Mark 33 was reputed to be a spy.

But no alarm rang and they were soon safely in two bins on the waste truck.

* * * *

Peter sat in the darkness. He reckoned from the bumping of the truck they were about at the gate of the school. This was the moment. Would the truck be searched? It stopped. He could hear voices. Then the truck went on again. They had made it.

The truck went on for what seemed like half an hour. Then it stopped. The lid was taken off his bin. It was John. They leapt off the truck and ran down a street.

* * * *

They wandered round the town all morning. At first they were frightened by the noise of the traffic but, as they got used to it, they could take in the sights of the city: the different coloured clothes instead of everybody being dressed the same; the prettiness of the girls; the goods in the shops; the relaxed look in people's faces.

By 1200 they were hungry. This was their problem. They

had no money to buy food. If they were going to survive in the Outside they had to have money. No real money was used in the school. Here they could see it being used in shops.

* * * *

They went into a park. It was beautiful. The sun shone. Ducks were on the lake. Girls in pretty dresses laughed and giggled. They sat on an empty bench to consider their next move. Opposite, men sat reading newspapers which looked different from the Party News which they had to read at school.

'We must steal some,' said John.

'Let's try and borrow some first,' urged Peter.

'It could give us away,' said John.

'Let's risk it,' said Peter. 'Please. I can't steal.'

'All right,' agreed John.

They approached a man reading a newspaper. Peter coughed. 'Excuse me, sir,' he said. 'My friend and I have no money for a meal. Could you lend us some?'

The man put the paper down slowly. It was Meakins. 'I want no fuss,' he said. 'Just move slowly to that car by the gates. You are watched on all sides.'

* * * *

Peter was now fifteen. At the back of his mind he had a certain kind of fear which he could not explain. But at the front of his mind he knew only love for the Party. His best friend at the school was Meakins, Leader 21. He was helping Peter to get an important job in the Ministry of Taxes when he left. He guided him in all things. Peter had an extra job, too: to find out any boys who did not love the school and the Party and to give their names to Meakins.

John 24 was with him as he jogged round the track on a voluntary extra session before bed. 'Watch Stephen 17,' said John. 'He did not take his B4 this morning'.

'I shall feel proud to,' said Peter.

Think It Over

What was the name given to a special group?
What happened at talk time?
What was the name of their leader?
How long had Peter been in the school?
Why would he be able to work in the Ministry of Taxes?
Why were they glad when the light on the TV went out?
What is the 'Outside'?
What surprising news did John tell him?
How did they know there were girls beyond the steel fence?
How did they plan to escape?
What had they to do in the school, if they couldn't sleep?
What did Peter want to do, if he escaped?
How had Mark 33 changed when he had been recaptured?
Why could the boys talk while they were having showers?
How did John get round not being able to talk to Peter?
What were they doing just before they made their escape bid?
How did Peter guess that they were at the gates of the school?
Name three things that surprised them about the city.
What main problems did they discover?
Who was the more honest of the two and how do you know?
How do you know they never really escaped?
What kind of people had Peter and John turned into at the end?

Do You Know?

Why might the story be called 'The Greenhouse Children'?
Why might Peter be No. 33?
What sort of Party was it? Name three kinds of Party in this country now.
Would you have liked Peter's school? Why?
What do we call the Ministry of Taxes now?

What kinds of places have electrified fences round them?
Have you ever seen one? Where?
Why might the girls' school be separate?
What is a medicine ball? Can you eat it?
Why are the children separated from their parents?
What kinds of people nowadays use hidden microphones to listen to other people's conversation?
Why were the Greenhouse Children made to run on the track?
Do you take any exercise? Why? What sort of things do you do and when?
What is a blind spot?
Why might the Outside newspapers be different?
Why does Meakins want no fuss when he arrests them?
Is it sometimes necessary to give away a secret or report someone? When? What are your views?

Using Words

Invent some code names for food you ate yesterday.
'monitored'. What is a simpler word? Make a list of words ending in *or*.
Write out the time for 0715 hours and 2345 hours.
'compound' List six *com* words with one *m* and six words with a double *m*. Use a dictionary.
'The word had hit him like a medicine ball in the stomach.' Write this suggestion of shock in your own words.
'Rumour had it'. What does this mean?
'reappeared' Write down six words in which *re* is added to another word.
'play safe'. How many other sayings can you think of which use the word *play*?
'John had worked out'. Use 'worked up', 'worked through', 'worked over' in sentences of your own.

'They had made it'. What does this mean?
Use these words, correctly spelt, in sentences of your own:
  knowledge, medicine, disappear, criticism.

Write Now

In play-form write the conversation Peter's mother and
  father might have when he is selected for the school.
You are stranded in a strange town without money. Write
  what you would do.
You are Meakins. Write a report of a day in your life at the
  school.
Describe in detail what happened to the boys when they
  were caught.
You are sent to this school or to the girls' school next door at
  your present age. Describe your immediate impres-
  sions.
List the things you would most miss about the Outside, if
  you were in this school.

How Pecos Pete Became A Preacher

Pecos Pete came riding across the Yellow Badlands like a bat out of hell. The desert wind had been blowing all day. It had been lashing dust into his skin and eyes. It had been blowing hard enough to skin a cat. But it wasn't the wind that stopped him.

'Whoa!' said Pecos Pete and pulled his horse up in a skitter of stones. He looked all round. There was nothing to see but sand. There were a few rocks. None of them were big enough to hide a rattler. Pecos stared about him suspiciously.

'Too much sun,' he told himself. 'I'm getting round to imagining things.'

'No, no,' the Voice disagreed. 'No, you're not.'

'I'm going loco!' Pecos gasped. Trembling, he took the bottle of Old Redeye Whisky from his saddle roll and threw it on the ground. It smashed. He swallowed, shaking his head sadly.

'You're not mad, I assure you,' the Voice insisted.

'Tarnation!' shouted Pecos. He glared around, his gun in his fist. 'Come on out of it, you critter, or I'll blast you! I can see you!'

'Now, you know that's a lie,' the Voice said gently. 'Let me explain.'

* * * *

Pecos slid dizzily off his horse and leant against it, shaking. He gulped, unable to speak.

'I am,' said the Voice, 'inside you. I am using you as a host body. I hope you don't mind. I had to, you see.'

Pecos Pete's mouth opened and closed like that of a fish. No sound came out of it.

'I am from another planet,' the Voice went on. 'My ship, my transport, landed not far from here and I set out to explore. But I had not reckoned on the wind. It blew me along. I was knocked into something. My space suit failed. I had to seek shelter quickly. Luckily, you came along. My race, fortunately, can use your race as host bodies. Indeed, you saved my life. I am most grateful.'

'What d'you mean – "inside me"?' Pecos growled. It was the only thing he had understood.

'Oh, dear!' said the Voice. It began to explain again. It was a being from another planet. It had landed on Earth to take a look round. It had left its space ship and been carried away by the wind. It was only small. Its space suit had been damaged and it had feared for its life. Fortunately, being small, it could live inside other life forms. It had seen Pete coming along on his horse and taken its chance. Once inside a human being it could read his thoughts and talk his language.

* * * *

'It doesn't have to be a human being,' the Voice said. 'I could have lived inside the horse. But you seemed at first glance the more intelligent.'

'Thanks,' Pete said absent-mindedly. 'You're – you're kinda inside me then, eh? Where did you say you came from?'

'I'll try once more,' the Voice said patiently and went through the whole thing again. In the end, Pete seemed more or less to understand.

'How long do you reckon on staying inside me? he asked.

'Just until I can get back to my ship. I can transfer to it immediately.'

'And where's that?'

'I'm not sure,' the Voice said. 'The place seemed to be inhabited. There were buildings about. I thought they were buildings. Men like you were walking about. The buildings were brown.'

'I guess that's Dead Man's Gulch,' Pete said, 'That's where I was headed.'

'Splendid!' exclaimed the Voice. 'I would be most grateful.'

'You're mighty welcome, stranger,' said Pete.

'Oh, I am relieved!' the Voice gasped. 'You *are* a good man!'

'I try to be,' said Pete modestly. 'Matter of fact, my Maw always wanted me to be a preacher. Never got round to it, though. Somehow with all the gambling and fighting and drinking I was doing, there never did seem enough time to take up preaching.' He thought for a moment. 'I got to warn you, though,' he said. 'There could be a mite of danger in it for you.'

* * * *

'Danger?' said the Voice.

'Yeah,' said Pete. 'I was playing cards last night in Salt Flat City. Playing cards with Black Jack Daniels. It turned out that I had four aces and he had four aces, too. Sure looked like one of us was cheating. I didn't stop to argue. Black Jack is the fastest gun this side of the Swiftwater. I couldn't hit a barn door, standing next to it. I reckon Black Jack is looking for me. I was just going to stop over in Dead Man's Gulch for some grub. Then I'm riding right on out again. Fast as I can. I reckon if I get shot, you get dead right along with me, don't you?'

'Oh,' said the Voice.

'Still want to stay with me?' Pete asked.

'I really haven't any choice.' The Voice sounded much less grateful.

'There's just one thing,' Pete said.

'What?'

'Well – like you being from another planet and all that – you might have ways of helping me to beat Black Jack. You'd be doing me a mighty good turn if you could help me to outdraw him. Being inside me and all that.'

'No,' snapped the Voice. 'My race of beings do not approve of any kind of violence at all.'

'Shucks!' groaned Pete. 'This sure enough ain't my day. Giddap, horse!'

* * * *

They rode the next two miles in silence. Pete stopped at last.

'That there is Dead Man's Gulch,' he said. 'Is that the town where you landed?'

'Yes! Yes!' the Voice said excitedly. 'Take me into it. Quickly! Please!'

Pete shrugged and rode into town. The weather-beaten buildings closed in on him. The tumbleweed blew down the street. The place seemed strangely empty. In the next moment, he knew why.

Facing him, in the centre of the street, stood a figure in black. Pete knew that thin black moustache; he knew those deadly eyes. He stared at that cruel hand twitching above the gun in the gun belt.

'Black Jack!' he gasped.

'Correct!' hissed Black Jack. 'I'm aiming to kill you for cheating. Get down off that horse. I don't aim to damage the animal none.'

* * * *

Cold with terror, Pete slid off the horse's back. And then things happened too quickly for him. He had to work it all out afterwards.

As Black Jack's hand became a blur, Pete's own arm was seized by a strange force. His gun was out and firing before Black Jack's 45 had cleared its holster. Black Jack fired once. But by then he was rolling in the street and he had fired again and the black revolver flew yards away from Black Jack's hand. Then, moaning and clutching his leg, Black Jack gave up.

'The ship! My ship!' the Voice squeaked in Pete's head. Pete felt something like a wrench for a moment. Then the being was gone. A tiny silver thing soared up from beside the saloon and vanished in the pure blue sky. The Voice from another planet had helped him in the end. Now it had gone. Pete hardly noticed its going. He was thinking hard of something else.

* * * *

It didn't come back. Maybe it was ashamed of itself for using violence on Black Jack. Maybe it was just too scared to visit that neck of the woods again. Pete never heard from it after that. Neither did anyone else.

That was the end of Black Jack, too. In that flash of time, Pete—or the Voice inside him—had shot off both of Black Jack's boot heels. As he fell over, Black Jack had shot himself in the leg. A gunslinger who shoots himself with his own gun is a pretty comical fellow. And Pete had outdrawn and outshot him. Those who knew Pete claimed that that made Jack the slowest gun this side of the Swiftwater. It finished Jack, anyway. He gave up gunslinging for good. Last folks heard of him, he was selling ladies' hats in Denver.

* * * *

But Pete was not thinking of anything like this at the time. As he stood in the main street of Dead Man's Gulch with the gunsmoke curling round him, his mind was on other things. The dust blew past him and the tumbleweed brushed his legs. He did not move.

Black Jack had, indeed, been the fastest gun this side of the Swiftwater. And Pete had beaten him to the draw. That made Pete the fastest gun in the region. The news would travel. Then, every young cowboy with a gun would want to try his luck. Being fastest gun was like having a world title. Everyone wanted to be known as the fastest gun this side of the Swiftwater. Or—better still—as the fastest gun in the West. They would all be flocking round Pete like hornets round a sugar-cake. They would all call him out and challenge him to a gunfight.

Pete stood there in that dusty street and shuddered. He knew he would not stand a chance.

So, even before Black Jack had hung up his guns, Pete had

hung his up. That afternoon Pete bought himself a black jacket and a white shirt and a big black hat. From that day on Pecos Pete was a preacher.

He said it himself, one day after he gave a service in Tombstone. Being a preacher was kind of lonesome at times. It was mighty dull nearly all of the time. But you sure as hell did live a whole lot longer.

Think It Over

Why was Pete riding 'like a bat out of hell'?
What stopped him?
Where did he think the Voice was coming from at first?
Why did he destroy the bottle of whisky?
How was it that the Voice could talk to Pete?
Where had the Voice to get back to?
How do you know that Pete was very shocked?
What suggests that the Voice belonged to a very small being?
How might its space suit have been damaged?
Can it live in Earth's atmosphere? What makes you think so?
Who do you think was cheating at cards and why do you think so?
Why was Pete going to Dead Man's Gulch?
What makes the Voice less grateful to Pete?
Why was Black Jack so called?
How true to its beliefs about violence was the Voice?
Why does Black Jack become a laughing stock?
What turned Pete into a preacher?

Do You Know?

What sort of Country would the Badlands be? What kind of things might grow there?

What is a 'rattler' and why is it so called? How would you
recognise a poisonous snake in this country?

How does shock affect a person?

Pete thinks that the sun or whisky is making him imagine
things. What else might make a man see visions? What do
you call an imaginary vision seen in a desert?

What language would you most like to speak?

From what the Voice said, how else could it have avoided
danger?

How does the Voice's race differ from men?

What sort of things is the human body normally host to?

Why would the buildings in Dead Man's Gulch be brown?
Why would the street be dusty?

What sort of landscape would the river, Swiftwater, be
running through?

What kinds of seeds in England are carried by the wind?

Where is Denver? Can you name any towns that were famous in the American West?

Which world title would you like to have and why?

Why might being a preacher be a lonely job? Why would
Pete think it a dull one? Was he a suitable person to
become a preacher? Why?

Using Words

'I'm going loco'. What does *loco* mean? What is a *skitter* of
stones? What is a *gulch*?

critter imitates the way a cowboy would say the word. How
would you normally spell it?

Ask your teacher what a cliché is. How many clichés can
you find in this story?

'That's where I was headed.' How else could you say this?

'I would be most grateful' Say this more simply.

'a mite of danger' How big is a mite? Where does the word
come from?

'a mighty good turn' What word could you use instead of
   mighty. Write a sentence in which *mighty* is used in a more
   normal way.
'if I get shot, you get dead right along with me'. Would you
   say that? What would you normally say?
When Pete first heard the Voice he was am. . . . Supply the
   missing letters.
'I don't aim to damage the animal none'. Put this into
   correct, everyday English.
What does 'this neck of the woods' mean?

Write Now

Write a Western story in which a UFO saves some cowboys
   from the Indians.
Describe a very hot, windy day.
Make a list of things a cowboy might own.
'that cruel hand twitching'. Write a sentence or two describ-
   ing the hands, eyes and lips of a man about to attack.
In play form write the conversation some men in the saloon
   have about the fight and what happened afterwards.
Write a story about a boy in the West and his horse.
Describe your favourite cowboy character, or invent one.

Giant's Spit

Gary and Joy stood on the bridge of their small Yorkshire town looking at the river. 'It looks like spit,' said Gary. 'It looks like giant's spit.'

They were looking at the foam coming from the glue factory. It was floating down the river in great sponge-like lumps. The wind carried it on to the bridge. Some of it went on Joy's face. 'Ugh!' she cried. 'It smells.'

Gary teased her: 'You've got a moustache,' he said. 'The giant's spit has given you a moustache.'

Joy ran off to school. Gary followed. He told the other children in the playground about it. 'Giant's spit!' they chanted 'Giant's spit!'

* * * *

The parents had protested about the spit, especially as the children played by the river. But the council said that the glue factory meant a lot of jobs for the town. The spit was caused by chemicals from the waste being discharged into the river. The factory had tried to keep it to as little as possible but their glue was very popular and they worked 24 hours a day.

The mistake happened on the night shift. The brain does not work as well at night as man is a daytime animal. Like all mistakes of its kind it had more than one cause.

Down in the Midlands a man had loaded twenty drums of the wrong chemical on to a truck. He was a good workman but his wife had left him the day before and his mind was not on the job. That should not have mattered as all chemicals used in the factory were checked. But the man who should have checked them had not slept well during the day; he had

49

been disturbed by children playing. He had been to the pub on the way to work and had met some mates who had just come off the second shift. He had drunk too much and he arrived late and flustered. He was the man responsible for the mistake. He had poured the twenty drums of chemical into the vats.

* * * *

Gary and Joy were on the bridge next morning. 'The giant has spit a lot,' said Joy. They looked in amazement. A huge cloud of foam, some thirty feet high, was coming from the glue factory. More children joined them, excited by their shouts. People on their way to work stopped to look. The cloud of foam was approaching rapidly, blown by the wind. Instead of the normal pockets of foam it was one big continuous mass and it was growing and rising all the time.

The children and watchers were hypnotised by it. By the time they had decided to run it was over the bridge. It came over like a giant bubble bath. Some children began to cry as they could not find their way out.

* * * *

Gary had taken Joy's hand. A truck narrowly missed them and crashed over the bridge into the river. Further down the road another car crashed but the sounds of that and the other children were muffled by the foam. Joy was frightened as much by the silence as by the fact that she had lost her bearings.

Meanwhile in the glue factory the men had not yet realized what was happening. The foam was being driven down-wind from them.

From the hillside above the town people saw this growing mushroom of white. It quickly covered the town centre and reached half-way up the steeple of the parish church.

* * * *

Gary and Joy ran. They did not know where they were going. The foam seemed to be getting thicker all the time. The people in the buildings and shops suddenly saw their windows covered with the foam. They went to their doorways but quickly shut their doors as the foam blew in.

Gary and Joy suddently realized that they could not run as fast as they normally could. The foam now seemed to be clinging to them like slime. It was thickly coated on their arms and legs. Instead of being light and fluffy it was now sticky.

Have you ever walked in thick mud? Having to pull your foot out to make the next step? This was how they now walked. But it was also the same with their arms. They had to slide their arms out as well. What was happening?

* * * *

You must remember the spit came from the glue factory. A chemical in it was making it hard. It had begun to solidify.

There came that time when they could no longer pull out their arms and legs. They were stuck fast. Gary tried to get the pen knife out of his pocket but he could not reach it. They were stuck like flies in jam, able to wriggle a bit, but stuck firmly. It was like being stuck in polystyrene. They could breathe for so long because of the bubbles of air around them and in the spit. It was light too. But it was very silent.

Outside the area of spit the rescue attempt had begun. Bulldozers were being used to clear a way through but there were only three of them in the town. It would take many hours to get more. One of the dozers cut a man in half getting him out so the rescuers had to go very slowly.

Gary and Joy were exhausted by their efforts to make a bigger space round them. They were stuck there, holding hands.

* * * *

At school Miss Willis had arrive early and was seated at her desk, marking. She looked at the clock and was surprised there were no sounds of children playing in the playground. It was dark too. Perhaps there was a storm coming. At this moment the head cook rushed in, screaming. They went to the main door. Miss Willis tugged it open and touched a solid wall of white foam. They had no idea how widespread the tragedy was. Their only idea was to get out. They went to the kitchen for some sharp knives.

At the rescue headquarters a new danger was realized. The glue factory had told them that the spit was highly inflammable. None of the rescuers must smoke. They would just have to pray that no gas mains or electric wires were cut or fractured.

* * * *

Knives were not the right thing to cut the foam. They quickly blunted and had to be sharpened back in the kitchen. After two hours they had cut only four yards and it had exhausted them. Miss Willis sat down with one of the cooks. 'I must have a fag,' said the cook. She reached for her handbag.

'No!' said Miss Willis. 'It might foul the air.'

'But me nerves!' moaned the cook. 'Just a short drag.'

'No. We could be in here some time. We must not foul the air. What was that?'

* * * *

Gary and Joy were now both sobbing. They were also breathing more quickly as the air supply had begun to run out.

'There's a dog or something trapped just ahead of us,' exclaimed Miss Willis. She dug furiously and uncovered a hand. She had just missed cutting it with the knife. It was Joy's. Working feverishly they uncovered the two children and dragged them into school. Joy smiled as she saw Miss Willis. Gary had passed out but he slowly recovered back in school.

* * * *

They were in the school three days before they were rescued. When they were dug out Miss Willis was amazed at the extent of the tragedy. A large area of the town had been covered by the foam. Most people were safe because they managed to get into buildings. But some thirty people, including six children, died outside in the streets.

The miracle was that no fire happened. The fire chief said the town would have been a fireball if a careless cigarette had been thrown away. Luckily most people, thinking of their air supply, had not smoked.

The town is now back to normal—if you can ever be normal again after a tragedy like that. But the glue factory stands idle. The Council wants it to start up again. They say there are now safeguards to prevent that kind of thing happening again. But the people do not believe them. They do not trust scientists any more. There is a picket on the gates daily to prevent entry.

The river is now, therefore, clean and free of giant's spit. The children can play there safely again. That is all but six of them.

Think It Over

Where does the story take place?
Who invents the name 'giant's spit'?
Where was the spit coming from?
Why does Joy not like the spit?
Why do the parents protest about the spit?
Why does the Council do nothing about it?
What was the mistake?
How many men were involved in the mistake?
Why did the men in the factory not realize the danger at first?
What amazes Gary and Joy next morning?
What happens to the truck in the spit?
How high is the spit?
What change takes place in it?
What happens to Gary and Joy?
What helped them to breathe when they could no longer move?

What happened when the bulldozers tried to rescue people?
Why does the cook scream?
What is an added danger?
Why does Miss Willis stop the cook smoking?
How does Miss Willis rescue Gary and Joy?
Who had survived the imprisonment best?
Why were most people safe?
What caused the deaths of the thirty people?
Why do the people picket the glue factory?

Do You Know?

What usually causes foam on a river?
Are there any factories near you? Have there ever been any
    complaints about them? Why?
How old do you think Gary and Joy were? What makes you
    think so?
What is the best glue?
What did glue used to be made from?
What is the strangest sight you have seen?
Where might the bulldozers have come from?
How could the glue factory communicate with the rescuers?
What recent disasters have you heard about? Were any of
    them man-made?
Why might the Council have wanted the glue factory to start
    up again? What might happen in the town, if it were
    closed for good?
What factories are the most dangerous?

Using Words

Why is there an apostrophe in 'Giant's Spit'?
'discharged into the river'. What happens to a man, if he is
    discharged?

'the Midlands'. Where are they? What do you understand
    by 'the Home Counties' and 'the Black Country'?
'. . . had met some mates who had just come off night shift'
Complete these 'who' sentences:
    I know a boy who . . .
    They came upon a tramp who . . .
    There are some footballers who . . .
If you are rushed and worried, you are flu . . . . .
What is a vat?
'It came over like a giant bubble bath'. Think of another way
of saying this.
'she had lost her bearings'. Write this in another way.
'solidify' What single word means the opposite of this?
Why is a pen knife so called?
'They were stuck like flies in jam'. Think of another way of
    saying this.
'polystyrene' How many other words do you know that
    begin with *poly*? Can you find out what 'poly' means?
What is the difference between a gas main and a gas pipe?
'Gary had passed out'. Use one word for 'passed out'.
'fireball' Make a list of words beginning *fire*.
Use each of these words, correctly spelt, in sentences of your
    own: moustache, popular, tragedy, continuous,
    exhausted.

Write Now

Describe in a few sentences what it is like to walk through
    thick mud.
You are stuck in the giant's spit and rescued from it.
    Describe your experiences.
Write a poem called 'Polluted River'.
Describe a clean river on a summer's day.
In play-form write a conversation one of the families trapped
    in their house might have OR write the conversation
    between two rescue workers.

What things are there near you which are ugly or unpleasant and are caused by industry? Write a letter to the local paper complaining about them.

Have you ever made a serious mistake? What happened?

Write an account for a newspaper of some natural disaster and the rescue.

The Mind Of The Droogs

On the planet Arvarn, there is a tower of stone. It marks the place where the gods landed to save Ishtar and her people. The gods killed the dragon and drove away the demons. They freed Ishtar's people from their cruel slavery.

But it was not quite like that. Brand and his companions could tell the true story.

* * * *

They were an odd team. Brand came from Earth. Skrill came from a planet in another star system. Lurgath came from yet a different world. To Earth-eyes, Skrill looked like a huge man-wolf. Lurgath was a kind of octopus. But they had a lot in common. None of them liked safety and order and peace. All of them were—what? Pirates? Soldiers of fortune? Call them adventurers.

They were running short of fuel. Lurgath spotted the planet first. 'Down there!' he indicated. He did not need to speak. Lurgath had the power to contact all other minds. He could talk to them without speech.

'That planet?' Brand asked. He looked at the print-out on the computer. 'Yes, there could be fuel down there. The place is called Arvarn. It was colonised from Earth over four thousand years back. No high degree of civilisation yet. Reports say it was invaded by another race some time ago.' He read more of the details. 'You're right, Lurgath,' he agreed. 'There's nacronium on the planet. We can use that as fuel.'

'Nacronium and trouble,' Lurgath told him. He could sense it even from out in space.

'Trouble?' growled Skrill. He liked the idea.

Brand orbited Arvarn once and brought the space ship down in a perfect landing. Lurgath looked through the space port. 'The computer was right. There are Earth people here.' he reported. 'And there are other kinds of beings. Come and look.'

* * * *

Ishtar and her people were working in the fields. They stopped to look up as the bright thing fell from the skies. When it landed, they stood and stared.

The Droogs hissed at them and spat their poison. One of Ishtar's people died. The rest cowered and went back to work. A group of Droogs set out across the plain to the star ship.

'They're like huge insects,' Brand said as he walked to meet them.

'They're the masters on this planet,' Lurgath reported.

'I go fight them,' Skrill growled. 'Bite. Chop them up. Kill.'

'Not yet.' Brand stopped him. 'We need fuel. We'll talk first.'

The insect creatures came up and surrounded them. 'I am Droog,' said one. 'What is it you want in this world?'

'Nacronium,' he said. 'We need it as fuel for our ship.'

'So? You read thoughts, eh?' the Droog said. 'You, at least, could be useful to us. What will you pay for the fuel?'

'What are you asking?' Lurgath demanded.

'Bring them back to the city,' the Droog ordered. 'The Great One will decide.'

* * * *

As they travelled, Lurgath studied the thoughts of the creatures. He spoke at last to Brand and Skrill. But he spoke aloud and used Earth speech.

'They are all Droog,' he said. 'They all look the same and have the same name. And there is something strange about the way they think.'

'Robots?' Brand asked.

'No, they are living beings. But their minds—there is

58

something I do not understand, yet. I need more time to study them.'

When they reached the city, they were taken to a room underground and shut in. They waited in their prison for most of the day. Towards night one of the Droogs came to see them. He communicated with Lurgath.

'What did he say?' Brand asked in Earth speech.

'He will give us fuel,' Lurgath seemed amused. 'But you will have to leave me here in exchange. He likes the fact that I can read minds.'

'No,' said Brand.

'If you refuse,' Lurgath went on, 'the Droogs will kill you both. Perhaps they will kill you, anyway. You're an Earth-man. Skrill, too, looks very like a man to these Droogs. Earthmen are slaves here. The Droogs have killed hundreds of them in war—or just for sport.'

* * * *

'I show Droogs,' Skrill growled. 'I crunch this one up. I break down door. Then we fight.'

'There are over a thousand Droogs in this city,' Lurgath told him.

'Yes. Hold it, Skrill,' Brand warned. 'We still know nothing of the nacronium. Where is it kept? Have you found out?'

'I know something,' Lurgath told him. 'The Droogs take the nacronium from the earth. They purify it. It should be just right to use as fuel. They keep it in a storehouse here in the city. I cannot see just where it is. But it should be easy to find. It is a big building with a dome. The Droogs keep a guard on it.'

'Right,' Brand decided. 'If they like sport, we'll give them some. Tell the Droog this,' he said to Lurgath. 'Say that we like a gamble. Winner takes all. One of us will fight with one of their best. If we lose, they get you. They can do what they like with Skrill and me. But, if we win, they give us the nacronium and we three leave together.'

* * * *

Lurgath delivered the message. The huge insect-creature seemed to think about it. Then Lurgath reported. 'The Droog agrees. The fight takes place tomorrow. They will prepare an arena.'

Skrill growled with pleasure as the Droog left them.

'Good!' he said. 'I fight tomorrow. I kill biggest Droog there is, I kill ten—twenty Droogs easy.'

'Not you, Skrill.' Brand stopped him. Me. I'll do the fighting. You go and find the nacronium while I'm doing it. Most of the Droogs will be watching the contest. Your strength will be better used in fighting any guards and carrying the stuff to the ship.'

Skrill tried to argue but Brand was firm. The next morning Brand was led into the arena. Lurgath and Skrill were brought to watch. They were guarded. But, when the fight was about to begin, it was not hard for Skrill to break away and get out into the city. He dealt quickly with the Droogs who followed him. They were not too many. All attention was fixed on the arena.

* * * *

When Brand saw what he had to fight, he knew why. The Droog he faced was many times larger than any he had seen so far. It seemed to tower over the arena. It shambled forward with its huge, glittering eyes fixed on him. He knew what he faced. This was the Great One of the Droogs. This must be their king and leader.

Hissing, it made a sudden dart at him, its sharp beak clacking. He dodged and it turned to follow. As it spat poison, he sprang aside. Brand smiled grimly. The Droog was slow where he was fast. And he had a weapon.

They had left their hand weapons on the ship. But Brand had one hidden in his boot. It was an old, old Earth weapon, a long knife, a sword. He drew it from its sheath. It glinted in the sun as he faced the rush of the Droog.

* * * *

But he found that it could not wound those armoured

60

scales and those armoured legs. The battle went on. Brand struck and dodged and skipped aside. Once the great beak slashed his shoulder. Spray from a jet of poison burned his arm and his leg. But he was still too fast for the thing. And the Droog was too well-armoured for him to do it harm. Then he slipped.

He was close to the Droog as it turned. His fall sent him sprawling between its legs and under its body. The hiss it gave seemed full of triumph. Its huge bulk sank down to crush the life out of him.

Then Brand remembered an old Earth tale. He set the point of the sword against a chink in the armour above him and pushed. The weight of the insect-creature did the rest. the sword sank home to the hilt.

* * * *

Brand felt the death shudder run through the monster. He let go of the sword and leapt aside as the great body rolled on the ground. He scrambled to his feet and stood ready. But the leader of the Droogs was dead. He pulled the sword free and turned to face any attack from the watching Droogs. None came.

The Droogs were wandering away. They seemed dazed, unsteady, half-dead. Their movements were slow and without purpose. Brand joined Lurgath and they went to find Skrill. None of the Droogs they came across paid them any attention. Some of the Droogs they met were lying on the ground. Their legs were twitching feebly. Were they dying? Other Droogs were wandering away across the plain. They moved slowly and aimlessly.

It was Lurgath who understood. 'The Droogs were like your Earth insects,' he explained. 'You have what you call ants, don't you? And termites? They have a queen, a leader. For the Droogs that leader is the brain of the colony. You have killed the mind of the Droogs and left only the dying limbs.'

* * * *

Ishtar and her people had been left unguarded. They came to Brand and lay in the dust before him to do him and his companions honour.

'We thank you, Great Lord,' Ishtar said. 'We will build you a temple. You can live in it. We will feed you and worship you for ever.'

Skrill had come back from the space ship. 'Temples?' he asked. 'We have much fuel in tanks, now. Do you want temples?'

'Stay with us, Great Lord,' Ishtar pleaded. 'Live here with us in peace and safety.'

Brand looked at her. Ishtar was beautiful and her eyes were kind.

'Peace and safety?' He grinned at her. 'I don't think I'm old enough yet for that kind of thing,' he said.

Ishtar and her people watched sadly as the silver star-ship arced its adventuring way into space. It was on the spot where the motors had burned the ground that they built the monument to the dragon-slayer.

Think It Over

Why did Ishtar and her people erect the tower of stone?
Who were the three members of the team?
Which one looked like an octopus? What was his special gift?
Why did they have to land on Arvarn?
Why did the idea please Skrill?
How long had the Earth people been on Arvarn?
What happened when Ishtar's people stopped work?
What did the Droogs look like?
Why did Brand stop Skrill fighting them?
What payment did the Droogs want in exchange for the fuel?
How did Skrill react to that?
How did Lurgath know where the storehouse for the nac-
    ronium was?

What did Brand offer in exchange for the fuel?
Why was it Skrill who went to find the nacronium?
Which of the Droogs did Brand have to fight?
    What was different about that Droog?
What were Brand's advantages in the fight?
Why did the Droog hiss with triumph?
What finally killed it?
Why did the other Droogs not attack?
Why did Ishtar and her people want Brand and his friends to
    do?
Why did Brand refuse?

Do You Know?

Where is your nearest tower? What tower have you seen that
    is not a church tower?
How many legs would Lurgath have had?
What monument to war stands in Whitehall?
Name a hero of legend who killed a dragon.
What sort of soldier is a soldier of fortune?
What sort of information, do you think, was stored in
    Brand's computer?
Name two fuels most important to our civilisation. Which
    fuels are in short supply? What might be the fuel of the
    future?
What is an orbit in space-flight terms?
What do you call a person who can read other people's
    minds? Would you be popular, if you could read other
    people's thoughts? Why?
How, in the Bible, did David kill the giant Goliath?
What is the biggest insect you know? Name an insect that
    uses poison to catch its prey.
How do you know that Brand was fairly confident about his
    ability as a fighter?
Would you have gone with Brand and his friends or would
    you have stayed on Arvarn? Why?

Using Words

What would be the twelve most useful words in a language?

What is a print-out from a computer?

If a window on a space-ship is a space port, what is a window on a ship?

Without looking at the story, punctuate this: They're like huge insects brand said as he walked to meet them they're the masters on this planet lurgath reported I go fight them skrill growled bite chop them up kill

Now check with the passage.

'tower' is used in two different ways in the story. What are they?

'The Great One'. Why do these words have capitals?

What words describe the Droogs when the Great One has been killed? Use two of them in sentences of your own.

'Hold it, Skrill.' What is another way of saying this?

What do you call the men who fought in the arena in Roman times? Check the spelling.

'Brand was firm.' Explain this.

'the star-ship arced its . . . way into space.' What does the word *arced* tell you about the way it flew?

'honour' List some silent *h* words. (Some begin with *w*.)

Write Now

Invent two interesting creatures with whom you would like to explore strange planets and describe them.

Draw a Droog and Lurgath.

Write the story about Brand's next adventure with his companions on another planet or in space.

Write a poem called 'Ants'. It could be funny.

Find out something about an interesting insect colony and write an article about it.

The Green Slime

The army unit had surrounded the field. The officers were tense and excited. Above flew three helicopters. They had the best sight of the object that had landed in the field. It was about forty metres long, cigar-shaped, and it glowed a bright green of diamond intensity.

Tanks were coming from a nearby army base but they had not yet arrived. The officers would feel better when they were there. More air cover was expected at any moment. But the first helicopter was radioing down: 'Movement from UFO. Hatch opening.'

* * * *

The officers watched from their armoured car. A bright green object like slime was oozing out of the hatch at the top of the UFO. It was moving at incredible speed. It spilt over the side, gathered itself up into a ball about two metres high, and rolled towards them. A second and a third mass of slime followed, each rolling itself into a ball.

The men fingered their guns nervously. 'Hold your fire!' barked one of the officers. But more and more masses of green slime came out of the UFO and rolled across the field. One soldier lost his nerve and fired; he was followed by another and a volley of shots rang out despite the shouts of the officers.

* * * *

The gunfire made no difference to the green slime. It quickly surrounded the armoured car. The next thing was amazing. The slime spoke. And it spoke in a cultured English. 'Your guns cannot kill us,' it said. 'We come in peace. Put away your guns; they can harm neither us nor our ship.'

65

The captain went white. 'Hold your fire, men,' he said. 'What do you want?' he said, feeling foolish as well as afraid. He could see no face, just an ugly lump of slime.

'We come to help your planet,' said the biggest lump of slime. 'Take us to your leaders.'

* * * *

The captain was wary. 'What leaders?' he asked, hoping the tanks would arrive.

'Your Prime Minister and Government,' said the slime.

'You cannot see them,' he said. 'Give your message to me.'

'We must insist,' said the slime.

'No,' said the captain. He was a brave man.

A small spurt of green spray shot from one of the balls of slime and covered the captain from head to foot.

'Certainly, sir,' he said. 'Follow me.'

* * * *

The armoured car set off for London. The green slime followed rolling fast. The army was now on full alert and this strange procession was stopped at several road blocks. Each time the green spray opened the road blocks as if by magic. A news flash had brought people out onto the streets. By the time the convoy had got to London there were thousands in the streets.

As no harm had been done by the slime and it was well away from its ship the Prime Minister's advisers said he could talk to it. It oozed its way into No. 10 Downing Street.

* * * *

'We offer peace to your planet,' it said. 'Your world is rent by many conflicts. We offer you peace.'

'How can you solve a problem we have not solved in centuries?' asked the PM.

'More ships will come and put the green gas into your atmosphere. Once breathed by you it will take all your aggression away. You will always have peace.'

'This is not a matter for just this country,' said the PM. 'It is a matter for the world.'

* * * *

The slime was flown to New York. All the countries in the world sent a delegate there to the UN. The big countries asked this question: 'What would a country do that had been invaded?'

'No country would want to invade any other,' replied the green slime.

'What would a man do who had his property taken?'

'No one would want to own property for himself'

'But it is man's nature to fight to survive.'

'You could poison us with your gas.'

'We live for many thousands of years.'

'The big countries were suspicious but the smaller countries were interested. 'What about our food?' they asked.

'The green gas would quadruple your crops and improve your weather.'

* * * *

The UN went into a month long debate while the green slime waited. In the end the vote was cast for the green gas.

'We are delighted to have helped you,' said the slime, 'but there is just one thing. We do not know what change it might have on you. You could come to be like us.'

A look of horror filled the faces of the delegates. 'Look like you?' they gasped. 'Never. We must never look like you. Man is a handsome noble creature, the lord of creation.'

A liquid oozed from the slime; it was like tears although it had no eyes. 'We have tried,' it said. 'We have tried to help your planet. When the last man on this planet is dying, he will think about us.'

The slime was flown back to its ship. It took off swiftly. Nothing like it was ever seen again.

Think It Over

What had landed in the field?
What kind of help was the army waiting for?
What were the first signs of life on the UFO?
What came out of the UFO?
How many 'creatures' were there altogether?
Why did the soldiers fire?
What effect did the gunfire have on the green slime?
What was the most surprising thing about the slime?
Why did the captain feel foolish?
When the green slime asked to be taken to the Prime Minister at first, what did the captain do?
How did the green slime get its way?
What offer did the green slime make to the Prime Minister?
What reply did he make and what happened after that?
What effect, apart from making him peaceful, would the green gas have on a person?
How did the United Nations vote at first about the green gas?
What made them change their mind?

Do You Know?

How are UFO's usually described in reports of sightings?
What sort of place is an army base?
What does 'air cover' mean?
What kind of plant is the green slime that normally covers ponds?
Why would gunfire have been harmless to the green slime in the story?
Who has the most cultured voice you know?
How many pips does a captain have on his shoulder?
For what reasons does a person's face go white?
What might the captain have had in mind when at first he

did not agree to take the green slime to the Prime Minister?

How, do you think, did the green slime open the road blocks?

Where is No. 10 Downing Street? Who lives there?

Do you think it possible for all nations to live in peace? Why? How could it happen?

Would you like to live for thousands of years? Why?

Why would the big countries have been suspicious of the green slime's offer?

Why would the smaller countries have been interested?

Are good looks very important? Why? Are other things more important? What?

What do the last words of the green slime suggest about the future of the human race?

Using Words

What is an army unit? What does *unit* usually mean?

'of diamond intensity' Why *diamond*?

Make a list of words describing a bright light. (A thesaurus would help.)

'barked one of the officers' What does *barked* suggest about the way he spoke?

Use 'neither—nor' correctly in a sentence of your own.

What does 'Prime Minister mean?

Without looking at the story punctuate the following: your prime minister and government said the slime you cannot see them he said give your message to me we must insist said the slime no said the captain he was a brave man Now check with the story.

'rent by conflicts' Give another word for *rent* in this case. What else does rent mean?

Use the following words, correctly spelt, in sentences of your own: incredible, surrounded, procession, aggression, suspicious.

'dying' How many words ending *-ying* can you list?

Write Now

Write a story about rescue by a helicopter.

Write a TV commentary for the programme which reports the coming of the strange cigar-shaped space ship and the appearance of its occupants.

In play-form write the conversation the Prime Minister might have with his advisers before deciding to talk to the green slime.

Describe the sight in the streets as the strange convoy reaches London.

In play-form the slime gets back to its own planet and reports about Earth to its leader.

Write a poem called 'Creature from Space'.

Dolphins

John Francis liked dolphins. They were his life's work. And he had come to hate it. He sat in front of the translating machine and thought.

He had been a small boy when he had seen his first dolphin. It was the main attraction of the pool. It could leap through hoops. It could catch a ball. As it finished each of its tricks, it would come to the side of the pool. The trainer would give it a fish. It popped its head out of the water and, as gently as a lamb, it took the fish from his fingers. John had been fascinated. You could say he had fallen in love with dolphins. They seemed such cheerful animals. He liked their stubby noses. He liked their small, twinkling eyes. He liked the noises they made. They seemed to him like yelps of joy.

* * * *

He read every book he could about dolphins. He found out that a dolphin's brain is bigger than a man's. A dolphin can tackle a shark and kill it. It charges the shark with its blunt snout. If a dolphin is wounded, other dolphins will gather round it to help it. Dolphins take good care of their young. Some of them take a friendly interest in men. There are tales of dolphins having helped swimmers in difficulty.

In his teens he got a job in a dolphinarium. That is a place where dolphins are kept in captivity and taught tricks. But he soon grew tired of that. He did not want to be the man who just made dolphins perform. He wanted to know about dolphins. He was clever and he could work hard. So, he took a degree in zoology and then specialised in the study of dolphins. It was not too hard for him to become a world expert in the subject. He had a talent for dolphins. That is how he came to work for the government.

* * * *

He was given all the help and equipment he wanted. There was a huge pool at the place where he worked. It was a large one so that it could be like a dolphin's natural home. There was a big underwater gate that led out into the sea.

At first he had thought he was the luckiest man in the world. He had the money he needed. He had a staff of people to help him. And, of course, he had the dolphins. He could put on a wet suit and swim with them. The dolphins enjoyed playing games with him. They were almost human. Almost? Sometimes he thought they had senses which human beings did not have.

* * * *

Times changed. He grew older. His work grew more important in the eyes of the government. He had to attend meetings. Much more of his time was spent in his office or his laboratory. He was not too fond of the laboratory. Experiments were performed there on dolphins. Sometimes the dolphins died. Dolphins had to be caught and brought to the pool for study. Sometimes some of these died, too. Some died because they were injured when they were caught. Others seemed to miss the sea so much that they fretted and died of grief in the pool.

John Francis began to regret his interest in dolphins. Perhaps these cheerful, bouncy creatures would have been better off if they had not attracted the interest of man. But he stayed at his work. One very special reason kept him there.

* * * *

Dolphins can talk to each other. Men, before John Francis, had come to have some understanding of dolphin language. But it is a difficult job. A man's ear can only hear a certain range of sound. The dolphins can make sounds so high that a human ear cannot catch them. So man's understanding of dolphin talk was very crude and incomplete.

John Francis wanted to understand them completely. It was a task that he worked on for years. Towards the end, though, he nearly gave it up.

The government's interest in dolphins had grown. Dolphins could be trained. They could do difficult and dangerous jobs underwater. They could do them well. The jobs could be so dangerous that they killed the dolphin. But dolphins do not complain. Dolphins could be trained for war. They could be trained to hunt out submarines. They could be trained to carry bombs to their deadly destination. The dolphins had done these things in practice. They had not seemed to mind. But John Francis had minded very much. He had hated to see these jolly, intelligent creatures used for killing.

* * * *

He had protested. He had written to politicians. He had written to the papers. He had even bought time on television. It had taken nearly all the money he had. He had put out his own programme. It had made no difference. The men in power had gone on having dolphins trained for war. To them he was just a fool, soft-hearted and probably a bit soft in the head. In the end he had had to admit defeat.

He was alone in the research station. It was nearly midnight. His window looked out over the pool. He had written out his resignation. It lay on his desk. He could not stop the evil things that were being done to dolphins. But he would be no part of it either. There was one last thing to do.

* * * *

His translating machine had never been a complete success. Yes, he could talk to dolphins. The machine could pick up the high sounds they made and turn them into human speech. He could speak into a microphone and the machine would turn his words into the inaudible squeaks of dolphin language. But all his conversations with the creatures were still simple. A life's work. And it had come to nothing, after all. He switched on the machine.

'Neptune,' he said. He could hear the noise of dolphins in the pool outside. He could hear their whistling and a noise like human laughter. Neptune was a dolphin he knew well. To John Francis he had come to be almost a person, wise and friendly. John Francis had worked with the dolphin, Neptune, to understand the dolphin speech. Neptune had seemed to understand what he was trying to do.

'John?' The machine translated the sounds the dolphin made.

'Tonight, Neptune,' Francis said, 'I am going to set you all free.' There were seven other dolphins in the pool beside Neptune. 'It is time to say goodbye.'

'Goodbye? Why "goodbye"?' The voice was flat and metallic in the machine. But Francis thought he could tell how Neptune felt.

'I am leaving here. I shall not speak to you again,' Francis told him.

'Leaving? No! Why?' the machine translated.

'Men are doing evil things to dolphins. I shall not help them any longer.'

'Not your fault, John. You are a friend.'

'I'm sorry, Neptune.' Francis found it difficult to speak. 'Goodbye,'' Francis repeated.

'Wait. Don't go. We have been friends. I want to warn you. To tell you of dolphins' plan.'

* * * *

'Plan?' Francis's hand, about to switch the machine off, stopped in mid-air. He could hear splashings out in the pool and louder whistling and shriller sounds. It almost seemed as if the dolphins were quarrelling. He waited.

'Other dolphins,' Neptune explained. 'They do not want me to tell. But I do not like the dolphins' plan. It is not kind.'

'What plan?' asked Francis.

'Man has owned the world for many, many years. Man has been very busy. Dolphins have not minded. Dolphins do not like to be busy like men. But lately man has been too busy. He has been killing too many things. He has killed very many whales. Whales are like dolphins. He has made his world dirty. Rivers are dirty. The seas are dirty. We know that many places on the land are dirty, too.'

'That is true,' Francis said.

'Many dolphins want to frighten man. They want to make him stop dirtying the world. A few dolphins want to take the world from man. They do not want to kill man. They want to take the world from him.'

'How?' Francis breathed.

'That will not happen,' Neptune told him. 'Most dolphins think that is a bad thing to do. But many dolphins agree to frighten man. That will make him kind to the world. He will be kind to animals. He will be kind to other men.'

'How are they going to do it?' Francis asked quietly.

'At the North Pole and at the South Pole there is much ice. Dolphins have found a way to melt that ice. The sea will rise over the earth. Some of the land will be covered.'

* * * *

Neptune stopped speaking. John Francis sat in silence. The dolphin said, 'John?'

'Yes,' Francis said. 'I'm still here.'

'The other dolphins said that I should not speak. But you have been my friend. Now you are leaving. I had to tell you. To keep you safe. You will warn other men. But I could not let you go without knowing.'

'Yes,' Francis said. 'Thank you. I am going to open the gate now. You can swim away to the open sea. Goodbye, Neptune.'

'Goodbye.'

Francis pressed the lever that opened the gate to the sea. But he did not move after that. He was deep in thought.

* * * *

He believed Neptune. Dolphins have a high intelligence. He knew that. They could change the seas. He had better report what he had heard. And what would happen then? The dolphins would be hunted down with ships and nets and bombs. He felt old and sick at heart. Then rage took him. He tore at the translating machine, ripping out wires and smashing tubes until it lay in ruins. But his rage passed.

Calm at last, he walked over to the telephone. But he did not lift it. He stood there a long time. Then he took his hand away, walked over to the switch and turned off all the lights in the room.

Outside the window the sea was silver in the moonlight. It gleamed clear and peaceful. Further up the coast there were factories but they were not near enough for their waste to muddy this stretch of sea. Not yet.

'No,' he said aloud. 'Let them find out. Let them find out as it happens.' And he walked out of the door into the night.

Neptune had waited until the lights went out. Then he turned and swam off into the freedom of the sea. No one else at the research station has heard from or seen John Francis since that night.

Think It Over

When did John Francis first take an interest in dolphins?
What tricks could the dolphins do?
What is the surprising thing about a dolphin's brain?
How do dolphins kill sharks?
Who have dolphins helped?
Why, at first, did John Francis enjoy working for the government?
Why did his attitude change?
Why did some of the dolphins die?
What special reason kept John Francis at his work?
What sort of things did he do to protest against the use of dolphins for war?
What final thing had he done on the night when the story starts?

What was the name of the dolphin he knew best?

How did the dolphin feel when John said goodbye to him?

How did the dolphin feel about men generally? How did he feel about John Francis?

What was the reaction of the other dolphins in the pool when Neptune mentioned the plan?

Why did the dolphins want to frighten the human race?

What happened to Neptune after he had revealed the plan?

What would happen to the dolphins, if Francis revealed their plan to his fellow men?

Why did he break the translating machine?

Why did he tell no one of the dolphins' plan?

Do You Know?

Where can you see dolphins in captivity in this country?

What kind of animal do you particularly like and why?

What other kind of animal can be trained to do tricks? Do you approve of teaching animals to do tricks? Why?

Where would you take a degree?

Where are dolphins found in nature? Are there any in the seas round this country?

What is a wet suit? How does it work? Can you name a man famous for underwater research?

Do animals have a language? Can pets sometimes understand what is said to them? Which creatures do you think are the most intelligent? Do you think animals have feelings? What has been your experience? Which creature would you like to communicate with?

Do TV programmes have much effect on what people think? Can you give any examples? What is the best way to make a protest to the authorities?

What other animals has man trained for war now and in the past? What do you think of training animals to be used in war?

A pagan god was called Neptune. Who was he?

Have you ever noticed pollution in the sea? Where? What caused it? What is the usual cause of pollution on beaches?

Was John Francis an evil man? What do you think?

Using Words

What is the difference between an aquarium and a dolphinarium?

'its blunt snout'. What other animals have snouts?

'as gently as a lamb'. What else could it be as gentle as?

'a talent for dolphins' What is a *talent*?

'cheerful'. Write down six other words ending in *-ful*.

What does *inaudible* mean?

'sick at heart'. What other expressions do you know with the word *heart* in them?

'it had come to nothing' Explain this.

Punctuate: i am leaving here i shall not speak to you again francis told him leaving no why the machine translated men are doing evil things to dolphins i shall not help them any longer

Then check your version with the story.

Use these words, correctly spelt, in sentences of your own: fascinated, laboratory, government, quarrelling, completely.

Write Now

Write your own story about a talking animal.

When the sea begins to rise who notices it first? Where does it happen? Write a newspaper account of the happening OR complete the story, dealing with the flooding of the Earth.

Write a poem called 'Submarine' or 'The Strange Sounds'.

Write a story in which you live under the sea.

What is it like to swim underwater, using diving equipment? Write an account of what you might see and do.

Come Back, Mr Wibley

Mr Wibley had a very respectable job with the local Council. I work for a weekly paper. When he went crackers, I went along to see him. I thought there might be a story in it for the national press. There was. But I can't see anyone printing it.

The home he was in was out in the country. He hadn't done anything violent. He'd been put in there for his own good. He was quiet and talked as reasonably as you or I. But when he started his story, I wondered. I asked him straight out about the flying saucers.

'Yes,' he said. 'They exist. I've talked to a creature who came to Earth in one. That's why I'm here. But you know that.'

'I know some of it,' I said. 'But I'd like to know more. That's why I'm here. What did it look like?'

'Can you imagine a sort of spider made out of green rubber with a trunk?'

'D'you mean a suitcase?' I asked, a bit surprised.

'Like an elephant,' he explained patiently.

These creatures wanted to make contact with Earth. They couldn't talk any Earth language, of course. But they could speak to the minds of certain people. There was the snag. They couldn't communicate with just anybody. Only with special cases. Mr Wibley was one of these. They had been trying to make contact for some time. But the people they had communicated with were a bit shy of admitting that fact to the world. Those who had admitted it, hadn't been believed. So, the saucer creatures had hit on a plan. They had given Mr Wibley proof that he had met one of them.

That was a sort of disc made of stuff like green glass. You held it to your forehead for a short time. The spider creature had told Mr Wibley that the disc would give him the power of flight. There was only one thing wrong with it. It didn't work.

'I know,' I said.

'I mean—it didn't work at first,' he explained. 'This green creature—let's call him Spido, shall we? Well, Spido talked to me by making pictures in my mind. I didn't understand him very well. I understood about the flying. But I found out later that there were a lot of Spido's pictures that I hadn't understood.'

'I see,' I said.

'I don't think you do,' he said. But I'll let him tell the rest of the story in his own words.

* * * *

'I tried the disc that evening,' he told me. 'I held it to my head for a good ten minutes. Then I went out into the back garden. I made sure no one was watching. I jumped up and down a bit. I even flapped my hands at my sides. Nothing happened.

'I must say I felt a bit relieved. I had met Spido out on the lonely moors where his saucer had landed. I was thinking about it, even then. I'm a quiet man. I don't like fuss. I didn't want to tell the world about flying saucers. People would want to question me. There'd be television programmes. Scientists would want to examine the disc. All that fuss. It made me feel quite hot under the collar. So I went back into the house. I'd been feeling tired all day, too. It was early. But I decided to have a bath and go to bed.

'That was weird. I was lying there in the hot water, whistling to myself. Suddenly I was bumping up against the ceiling. I realised then what Spido's mind pictures had meant. It was quite embarrassing. To fly I had to be whistling all the time. It had to be night time. The disc wouldn't work in daylight. It tried it afterwards. I had to be wet all

80

over. So, if I wanted to fly, it had to be raining. And I had to be stark naked. I checked that out, too.

* * * *

'Well—imagine! It put me right off. I couldn't see myself flying round town in the nude. I'd have to, if I wanted to demonstrate the disc. I went hot all over every time I thought about it. But Spido kept coming back into my mind. I thought of him and all the other creatures like him. I thought of them slaving away to make the disc. I felt I had a duty to Spido.

'So, one evening, when it was raining, I tried again. I waited until it was quite dark. Then I held the disc to my head, took off all my clothes and went out of the back door. I really felt a fool. I mean—I've got a bit of a stomach on me and I'm fairly bald. I wondered what people would say if they saw me. It was cold, too, with the rain dropping on my bare skin. But I set my teeth and started to whistle.

* * * *

'And it worked. It was marvellous. I went soaring up, keeping out of the lamplight and flew round the garden. I suppose I got a bit over-confident. I took a quick whizz round my own house. Then I flew next door. That was silly.

'I flew past the Wards' bedroom window. They hadn't drawn the curtains. Fat, old Mrs Ward was just getting into bed. She saw me at the same time as I saw her. Her mouth opened. I heard her scream, as I went zooming away to safety. Fortunately, I had thought to leave my bedroom window open before I started. I was through it like a rabbit down a hole. I was fairly trembling with fear. I knew Mrs Ward. She's very narrow-minded. I'd never hear the last of it, if she'd recognised me. Mr Wibley, stark-naked, peering in through her window!

* * * *

'I had a job getting into bed. It was a struggle getting my pyjamas on. I kept flying round the room. And even when I

as in bed and pinned down with the bed clothes, I kept
lifting off. The effect of the disc wore off after about an hour.
But it was nearly dawn before I got to sleep.

'I left the disc alone for weeks after that. Mrs Ward never
said anything. Perhaps she thought she had imagined it. But
she gave me some funny looks when we met in the street.
And yet—Spido was on my mind. The whole thing kept
worrying me.

'So I bit on the bullet at last. I made a plan. I'd go where
there were no people to see me. One stormy night, I got on
my bike and went up to the moors. I used the disc, took off all
my clothes and covered them with a bit of plastic weighted
down with a stone and started to whistle. I was off like a bird.

* * * *

'At first, I enjoyed it. It was cold and the pelting rain stung
a bit. But I liked soaring up. I even did a few stunts. What I
hadn't reckoned with, was the wind. It got stronger and I
had to go with it. And the power of the disc lasted for about
an hour. By the time I got down again, I had been blown
miles away from my clothes.

'Luckily, it was still dark. There was no one
about. I tore up a bit of bracken and used that to cover
myself with. But it was getting light by the time I reached my
bike and the clothes. And that wasn't the worst of it. The
wind had blown most of my clothes away. All I had left was a
pair of underpants. I stood there a long time, shivering and
thinking.

* * * *

'But there was nothing else for it. I got on the bike and set
off for home as fast as I could. But not fast enough. The town
had wakened up by the time I got there. By a great stroke of
luck I got to my house without the police stopping me. But I
cycled through streets of staring faces and one or two cat
calls all the same. The news got around quickly.

'When I got to work later, the Town Clerk called me in.
He talked of all the good work I had done for the Council.

But had I been working too hard lately? How did I feel? A bit strange? Had I ever thought I might need to see a doctor?

'Then it came to me Wasn't this the moment to break the news to the world? I told him the absolute truth. Somehow I managed to convince him. At least, I thought I'd convinced him. I told him about Spido and the disc and flying. I explained how it had to be night time, about how it had to be raining and all the rest of it. He seemed impressed.

'It was still raining outside. He suggested a test. I reminded him it had to be dark. He agreed to wait until then.

* * * *

'At about seven that night we all stood in the courtyard at the back of the Council Offices. The Town Clerk had the Mayor with him and two other men, all under their umbrellas. I don't know how many had stayed in their offices until after dark and were watching from the windows. I didn't know at that time that the two other men were doctors, either. I'd used the disc. I threw off my bathrobe and stood there stark naked.

'I shivered there in the pouring rain for one or two minutes. I whistled. I even flapped my hands a bit. But I didn't fly. What else could they think? After a while, the two doctors came forward and I ended up in here.'

He stopped. I closed my note book and smiled at him.

'Right ho, Mr Wibley,' I grinned. 'Very interesting.'

'You're the first person I've told the whole story to,' he said. 'I worked it out in the end. You see, I'd left the disc lying on the ground while I was flying round. Something in the rain must have damaged it. That must have destroyed its power. I didn't think it worthwhile telling the story in full before. But, since you asked. . . .'

'Fine. Yes. Thanks a lot, Mr Wibley,' I told him. 'Most interesting.' I said goodbye then and left him staring out of the window. And yet—he seemed so sane! I couldn't get him off my mind. I rang the home a day or two later just to ask how he was getting on. They told me he'd escaped.

* * * *

I went straight up there to find out more. And I did. One old lady told me a tale about the night before the escape. She had seen a thing hovering in the sky. It had landed on a hillside. Later she had seen a green thing hovering outside Mr Wibley's window. No one believed her, either. She was always seeing things.

A nurse told me about the escape. 'It was night,' she said. 'He must have got out of his room somehow. There he was in the middle of the lawn. It was pouring with rain. He was whistling. We ran out, calling to him. Then he was gone. He seemed to jump. We searched the grounds. But he wasn't there. We can't understand it.'

'No,' I said. I didn't try to explain. It didn't seem a very safe thing to do. Not in the home. But I knew. Spido had come back. He had given Wibley another flying disc and Wibley had used it well. What happened after that, I don't know.

Maybe he's gone off with Spido to some unknown planet. I hope not. That's why I'm writing this story. I tried to get the national papers to publish it. They laughed at me. They thought I was kidding. But I'll get it published somewhere, because there's something I have to say.

I want Mr Wibley to read it. I believe him now. And I want to say this to him.

Come back Mr Wibley, wherever you are. Come back and you and I together will tell the truth to the world. Together we will convince them that there are such things as flying saucers and flying discs. So—Mr Wibley—please come back.

Think It Over

What was the job of the man telling the story?
Where was Mr Wibley when the story begins?
What surprising thing did Mr Wibley believe?
What did the space creature look like?

84

How did it communicate with Mr Wibley?

What actual proof had it given him of its existence?

What power did this proof have?

When did Mr Wibley try it out? What happened at first?

What four things were necessary before the disc could work?

How did Mr Wibley find that out?

Why did he not try it again for some time?

What frightening experience did he have when he flew for the second time?

Why was it that Mrs Ward never spoke to him about it?

Where did Mr Wibley next try out the disc? What happened that time?

What was in the Town Clerk's mind when he asked Mr Wibley questions about his work?

How did the story-teller feel when Mr Wibley had finished his tale?

Who sees Mr Wibley's escape from the home? Why does no one believe her?

Why does the story-teller change his mind about Mr Wibley?

What happened when he tried to sell Mr Wibley's story to the newspapers?

Do You Know?

What sort of things does the local Council look after?

What is the national press? What is the name of your local paper? Do you think it is a good one? Why?

Who was Icarus? What did he try to do?

When was the first powered aeroplane flight? Who made it?

What is hang-gliding? What flying devices work by wind power alone?

Why might people who think they have seen flying saucers be a bit shy of saying so?

What sort of flying stunts might Mr Wibley have done while he was flying over the moors?

Why does he tell the journalist his story?

What had the old lady seen on the night of Mr Wibley's escape from the home?

What reasons might the journalist have for wanting to contact Mr Wibley again?

Using Words

The story refers to 'a home' into which Mr Wibley went. What sort of place was it?

'It made me feel quite hot under the collar'. Can you think of one word which means the same as 'hot under the collar'?

'weird'. How many words with *ei* in them can you think of?

'I went zooming away'. What does a plane do when it zooms? What does a television camera do?

Use 'quite' and 'quiet' correctly in sentences of your own.

How many ways are there of communicating with people?

Where will you find bracken? What does it look like?

Name six words that rhyme with *flight*.

Write Now

After Mr Wibley goes into the home, the Town Clerk's secretary feels sorry for him. In play-form, write the conversation she might have with the Town Clerk.

Write the story of what happened to Mr Wibley after his escape from the home.

You wake up one morning to find that you can fly. Are you pleased or scared? Where do you go? What difficulties and adventures do you have? Write an account.

In not more than a page, write a newspaper account of Mr Wibley's story.

A peculiar space creature suddenly appears in your local shopping centre on a Saturday. What does it look like and how do people react to it? What happens in the end?

Again

At the end of Earth time, there was still knowledge. War and many ages of mankind had spoiled the Earth. Mankind was coming to an end and the sun was beginning to die. But there were still space ships that could travel at almost the speed of light. There were robots that could think and act for themselves.

Man would still have to find a young planet on which humanity could begin again. None of the nearer stars had such planets. If there were such planets, they were many light years away from Earth. There were ways, however, to freeze a human body and keep it from harm. In that frozen sleep, a person would grow old slowly. So, the last of mankind made its plans for its survival. Then they sent out their star probes to distant and unknown worlds of hope. The passengers were small children. But the pilot was the ship itself. It had the brain to survey and to pick suitable planets. And it could do more than that. The journey would be very long. But, somewhere, mankind would go on.

* * * *

Attam and Effa did not feel the ship touch down. The robot ship had had its orders from the last of mankind back on Earth. It landed gently. It warmed Attam and Effa back to life. Then it spoke to them. When they heard its voice, they had to obey. 'Awake!' it ordered.

Attam opened his eyes and then Effa. They pushed back the clear screens that covered them and sat up.

'Hello,' said Effa.

'Hello,' said Attam.

'What are we doing here?' Effa asked.

'I don't know,' Attam told her. 'I can't remember much.'

'Neither can I,' said Effa. 'Not even any dreams. I've been so fast asleep.'

She had. It had been a safe and frozen sleep for very many years. Yet, even in that sleep, she and Attam had grown older. In Earth terms they would have both been nearly eighteen years old.

* * * *

'Where are we?' Attam asked.

'I don't know that, either,' Effa said. 'It looks pretty dull'

It did. Those who sleep through space and time do not need either bright colours or pictures in their ships.

'I'm hungry,' Attam said.

'So am I,' Effa agreed. 'Let's go and find something to eat.'

They got up and walked down the gangway between the two couches. The robot ship silently opened its door and let down a ladder. Effa halted in the doorway and gasped.

'Oh!' she breathed. 'It's lovely.'

Attam did not speak. He had never seen anything like it. Neither of them had. Or, if they had, they could not remember.

* * * *

They looked out on to a garden. It was green and growing. Brilliant birds skimmed the banks of brilliant flowers. The air was full of their song and distant streams made music. Slowly, hand in hand, with their mouths slightly open, they went down the ladder. With every step they took, they found fresh wonders. There were perfumes and all kinds of animals. There was fruit to eat. They ate and forgot their hunger. In that garden they were never to be hungry again. Together they walked among its murmuring leaves for hours.

The first violet evening came on. Then it was night and the stars appeared. Tired with their wandering and the marvels they had seen, they fell asleep.

* * * *

88

The next day was as happy as the first and the day after that. There seemed no end to the splendour of the garden. Time passed without sadness or care.

One day they went separate ways. Attam took one track, listening to the sounds of the garden and gazing at the trees and the animals. Effa took a different path. Something seemed to be taking her back to the ship. When she got near to it, the voice of the ship called to her and told her what she had to do.

Attam was sitting under a tree when she came to him.

'Attam,' she said. 'You must go back to the ship. It sent me to tell you.'

'Not now.' He smiled dreamily. 'I'm thinking up names for all these trees and plants and for any animals that I see.'

'But you must go,' she said. 'It wants you.'

So he went. Effa stayed in the garden. It still looked as pretty as ever but for some reason she felt sad.

* * * *

Attam reached the ship and the voice told him to enter. He climbed the ladder and when it told him to lie on the couch, he obeyed. He felt a touch like metal fingers on his head and fell into a half sleep. Then the voice began to speak to him and taught him many things. When it finished and he woke, he went slowly and thoughtfully back into the garden and found Effa.

'We must go,' he said seriously. 'There are many things we have to do. The voice in the ship told me.'

'Go where?' she asked in surprise.

'We must go out into the world,' he said. 'We've been happy here but only because we were ignorant. We have a new world to discover. It is our duty to work in it.'

'Work?' she said.

'We need to make ourselves clothes,' he explained. 'We'll make them from leaves first. Then, later, we can use other things. We need to make the things the ship has taught me about. We shall make fire. We shall use a thing called the wheel.'

'But I like the garden!' Effa protested. 'I don't want to leave.'

'We can't stay,' he said. 'It would be lazy.'

' "Lazy"!' she cried. 'What does that mean? We're happy here.'

'We have to go,' he told her. 'It is our destiny.'

'Destiny!' she said. 'I don't know what that means, either. It's just a word. And—look—the garden is here. It's real!'

* * * *

It was no use. Attam insisted that they had to go. The garden was in a high valley in a mountain range. When they reached the edge of it they looked out over a large plain. The low land looked a hard, cold place. There was not much green there. Effa began to cry.

'Stop it, Effa,' Attam ordered. 'You know we can't stay in the garden.'

'But I want to!' Effa complained. 'I hate leaving it.'

'We'll come back,' Attam consoled her.

But, in the years ahead, they had far too much work to do for that. They told the story of the garden to their children and their children, in turn, passed it on to their own children. Some of them even set out to look for the place. But, try as they would, none of them ever found that garden again.

Think It Over

What else was coming to an end besides mankind?
How had space ships and robots advanced by that time?
What was man looking for? What difficulties would he have?
How might the space travellers be able to reach faraway new planets?
What piloted the ship?

90

What wakened Attam and Effa? How long had they been
  sleeping?
How old might they have been when they left Earth?
What was the inside of the space ship like?
How do you know they were surprised when they saw the
  garden?
What was wonderful about the garden?
Who told Effa what she had to do?
Why did Attam not want to go back to the ship?
What did the robot tell him he had to do?
Where was the garden?
What did the land outside the garden look like?
Why did they never go back to the garden?

Do You Know?

What Bible story does this remind you of? In what ways does
  it differ from the Bible story?
How might mankind have spoiled the Earth? How many
  years do you think the Earth can last?
How fast is the speed of light?
What is a robot? What things that work a bit like a robot do
  you have in your home?
What would be the best colours inside a space ship for a long
  journey?
Why does freezing food preserve it? What other ways are
  there of keeping food fresh for some time?
What is the most beautiful sight you have ever seen?
Would you have liked the garden? Which do you prefer,
  gardens or towns? Why?
What colours can you see in a sunset?
What were the earliest clothes made from?
How could you make a fire, if you did not have any matches?
Do you believe in fate? Why?
What place would you most like to go back to and why?

Using Words

Make a list of words to describe pollution and make another list to describe a beautiful scene.

'many ages'. You have heard of the Iron Age or the Age of Steam. What would you call the age we live in now?

'unknown'. Give six words, beginning *un-*, which make an opposite.

'star probes'. What other meanings for *probe* do you know?

'Awake!' What would you have said?

Punctuate: what are we doing here effa asked i dont know attam told her i cant remember much neither can i said effa not even any dreams ive been so fast asleep
Now check with the story.

'I'm hungry'. How many phrases can you think of which mean the same thing?

'without sadness or care'. Give another word for *care* in this phrase.

In the passage which describes the garden, which do you think is the most descriptive sentence?

Use the following words, correctly spelt, in sentences of your own: separate, thoughtfully, remember, surprise, listening.

Write Now

Write your own story of two people who have to start life again on a new planet.

You are the last person to leave Earth. Describe your last days here.

Write a poem called 'Star Probe'.

You have been asleep for a hundred years. What kind of a world do you wake up to?

You invent your own robot. What kind of things can it do for you?